GREAT FRENCH PASSENGER SHIPS

WILLIAM H. MILLER

The
History
Press

For Margo Singagliese, who is very much like the great
French passenger liners – she too brings great charm,
beauty, style and, most of all, happiness into our lives

The mighty *Normandie,* quite possibly the most beautiful
Atlantic liner of the 1930s and perhaps the twentieth
century, arriving at New York's Pier 88. The towering,
83,000-tonner is being assisted by Meseck and Moran
tugboats. (Author's Collection)

First published 2014

The History Press
The Mill, Brimscombe Port
Stroud, Gloucestershire, GL5 2QG
www.thehistorypress.co.uk

© William H. Miller, 2014

The right of William H. Miller to be identified as the Author
of this work has been asserted in accordance with the
Copyright, Designs and Patents Act 1988.

British Library Cataloguing in Publication Data.
A catalogue record for this book is available from the British Library.

ISBN 978 0 7524 9152 3

Typesetting and origination by The History Press
Printed in India

CONTENTS

FOREWORD

I was born in Paris in 1930. My father was a well-recognised musician. He played the harp. He had gone to America on concert tours in the 1920s and early '30s, of course always by sea, and on board such French Line ships as the *Rochambeau*, *Lafayette*, *Champlain* and, of course, his favorite, the *Île de France*. He had vivid memories of these trips and especially those crossings. In 1937, he was offered a professorship of the harp at the prestigious Julliard School in New York City. Suddenly, but also excitedly, we prepared to leave Paris and move to Manhattan.

Finally, in September 1937, we were booked – sailing westbound from Le Havre on none other than the great *Normandie*. We were in fact 'emigrating' on the most luxurious liner of her time! But even greater good fortune awaited – my father was asked to give concerts during the five-day voyage and in compensation we were upgraded to first class. Could there have been anything more lavish than sailing to America in the high splendors of first class on the glorious *Normandie*?

There was absolutely nothing like the French Line and, of course, most especially the *Normandie*. Quite simply, the French liners were all very 'classy'. Once aboard, you felt you were in a part of France itself. They had this great, clearly discernible expertise in shipboard operation, in running what were some of the grandest floating hotels on the seas. French ships, I felt, had great, obvious ambiance plus the finest cuisine, the very best decor and some of the greatest examples of Art Deco afloat. They were so unique. More specifically, I always remember the bellboys, the muses, in their bright-red uniforms with gleaming gold buttons and their hats with the leather strap under the chin. French Line ships even smelled differently – usually of the finest of French perfumes.

My father continued to sail in the 1950s, usually on the *Île de France*. He never used either the *Liberté* or *Flandre*. Myself, I had only that one French Line crossing, but sailing on the *Normandie* has always been, well, my personal 'claim to fame'. There aren't many of us left these days!

I've known Bill Miller for almost fifty years. We share a passion for the great liners and have been long-time fellow members of the New York branches of the World Ship Society and Steamship Historical Society of America. Over the years, Bill has busily and joyously kept the liners alive through his lectures, his articles, pictures and films, but mostly through his countless books (over eighty to date, so I've heard). Myself, I am especially honored and grateful to be a part of this one, *Great French Passenger Ships*. Three cheers for the grand era of 'France afloat', for great ships such as the *Normandie* and *Île de France*, and for my good friend Bill Miller! Long may he continue to document the great liners.

Bernard Grandjan
Rego Park, New York, 2014

INTRODUCTION

The French, while all but gone from today's mega-sized international cruise business, created in earlier times some of the most noted, important and certainly style-setting liners ever to sail the seas. One only has to think of the *Île de France* and then even grander, the *Normandie*, as two of the ultimate Art Deco dreamboats. The beloved *Île* was the innovator, the starting point and great divide, of ocean liner style – after all, she introduced the new Moderne on the North Atlantic well before the 1930s. It was soon all the rage and would go on to influence not just passenger ships, but hotels, department stores, cinemas, railway stations, apartments, skyscrapers and even Hollywood. The *Île de France* was often described as a 'floating Ginger Rogers', referring of course to those highly memorable Astaire-Rogers musicals of the '30s.

The first generation of the British and German early super liners began at the turn of the century. French entrants came somewhat later, in 1912 and just two years before the start of the First World War. The splendid *France*, a 23,000-tonner with four funnels (the only French ship to have as many), was the great beginning. Successively larger and grander French liners would follow. The rest of the world soon began to notice, reaching a high point of blazing attention when the giant, speedy *Normandie* and Britain's *Queen Mary* fiercely competed in the late '30s.

There is no question about it; the French went on, from 1912, to create some of the finest interiors on the seas. In addition, their on-board kitchens and hotel service often garnered enviable reputations. It was said, even by the 1920s, that more seagulls followed the French liners than any others – the scraps of food were so much better!

The *France* led to the hugely popular *Paris*, introduced in 1921, and was followed in succession by the *Île de France*, two smaller liners (the *Lafayette* and *Champlain*) and, in glorious triumph, the magnificent *Normandie* in 1935. It was quite an evolution. But then also, even if less remembered, were the often eccentric-looking ships of Messageries Maritimes, which looked after the overseas colonies: in Southeast Asia, in the Indian Ocean and East Africa, and in the Pacific. (The French Caribbean outposts were looked after by the French Line in a sort of secondary Atlantic service.) Other French companies such as Paquet and Mixte served Africa as well.

As for France itself, the nation was derailed by the First World War and some historians say it was saved only by America's intervention in that devastating conflict. It did give rise, however, to the high pitch of the 1920s – the French rallied with advances in style, design, fashion and even bubbly imagery. Alone, the 'bright lights of Paris' became a great travel incentive. Then, like the rest of the world, the French plodded through the fatigue of the 1930s, the age of the Great Depression. Amidst harsh mass unemployment and long queues for food, there was, however, the occasional reason to cheer. *L'Atlantique*, said to be the most luxurious liner ever for Europe–South America sailings, was introduced in 1931 and was followed four years later by the aforementioned *Normandie*. Indeed, they were two of the most important liners of the twentieth century. But there were added occasions of sadness.

No less than four noted French passenger ships caught fire and burned out in the 1930s: the *Georges Phillipar*, *L'Atlantique*, *Lafayette* and *Paris*.

As with the rest of the world, the Second World War greatly disrupted the French liner fleet. The nation succumbed to Nazi invasion in June 1940 and then was itself divided by collaboration. Many French liners were forced into exile, serving the Allies under the Free French flag. By war's end in 1945, a third of the nation's passenger ship fleet was destroyed; the remainder scattered, disorganised, sometimes all but worn out. The French Line, with its premier run to New York, was greatly reduced, in 1945–46, to a pair of passenger-carrying freighters. From six grand liners there were but two survivors – the hard-worked *Île de France*, still needed for trooping until 1947, and the salvaged but moderately sized *De Grasse*. The French Line was a fraction of its former self.

The French were expectedly enthusiastic about post-war rebirth and rebuilding. In 1946, French Line headquarters in Paris buoyantly predicted the construction of as many as seven new liners, between 25,000 and 45,000 tons, for Atlantic service. In reality, they would build only two – the 20,000-ton sisters *Flandre* and *Antilles* – which were then divided: one for the New York run and the other for Caribbean sailings. There were fewer resources in post-war France and even fewer francs. There was no money to build a replacement for the stunning *Normandie*, but instead the former Nazi-German *Europa* had to be refitted as the national flagship. She was aptly renamed *Liberté* and recommissioned in the summer of 1950.

The colonial and especially the African services were reinforced with new tonnage well into the 1950s. They were much needed as vital links, for passengers as well as freight. But the end of the war also signalled the slow but steady death of the last French empire: among others, France lost Indochina, Suez and Algeria. By the 1960s, the old colonial and African liner services were breathing their last.

In the '60s, the French produced far fewer passenger ships. It was a nostalgic end of the line, with the creation of the *Ancerville*, *Renaissance*, *Pasteur* and, most notably, the legendary *France* of 1962. She sailed on the declining North Atlantic run, between Le Havre and New York, for only a dozen years before her vital subsidy from Parisian-based ministers was yanked. After more than 100 years, the French liner service to the New World had ended.

The last French-flag passenger ships were finished off themselves by the usual cluster of mounting problems: high operating costs, difficulties with seamen's unions, airline competition, the swing to containerised freight transport and a new generation of foreign-flag, multinational and less expensive cruise ships.

In this book, I choose to look over a century or so of French liners – from the four-funnel *France* to present-day cruising for French passengers, on board ships not under the Tricolor. From the past, it was a glorious cast, with ships such as the *Paris*, *Colombie*, *Aramis*, *Pasteur*, *Cambodge*, *Antilles*, *Ville de Bordeaux*, *Foch* and many more. These ships were part of a wonderful age and, I feel, well deserve another round of recognition.

Bill Miller
Secaucus, New Jersey, USA, 2014

ACKNOWLEDGEMENTS

Like the crew of a great French liner such as the *Normandie* and *France*, it takes many hands, a full crew, to produce a book such as this. First of all, the author is especially thankful to The History Press and its splendid team of editors for proposing this title and then producing it.

First class thanks to Anton Logvinenko for creating the colorised view of the *Liberte* for the front cover and to Stephen Card for his very fine painting of the *Champlain* on the rear cover. Great thanks also to my dear friend Bernard Grandjany for his evocative Foreword and to Michael Hadgis for his technical assistance. Equal thanks to several fine ocean liner collectors – Ernest Arroyo, the late Frank Cronican, Richard Faber, the late John Gillespie and Albert Wilhelmi – for providing fine, often unpublished photos from their extensive collections.

Further appreciation to Philippe Brebant; Michael Cassar; Luis Miguel Correia; the late Alex Duncan; Frank Heine; Dodhan Huros; the late John Havers; the late Andy Kilk; Arnold Kludas; Norman Knebel; Anthony La Forgia; Fred Rodriguez; Captain J F Puyvelde; Jurgen Saupe; the late Roger Scozzafava; the late Antonio Scrimali; Roger Sherlock; Don Stoltenburg; and V H Young & L A Sawyer. Companies and organisations that assisted include the French Line; the Halifax Maritime Museum; Med Sun Lines; Moran Towing & Transportation Company; Port Authority of New York & New Jersey; Port of Le Havre Authority; the Steamship Historical Society of America,; World Ocean & Cruise Liner Society; and the World Ship Society.

If the author has overlooked anyone, he extends a sincere apology.

1

THE NATION'S FIRST SUPER LINER: THE *FRANCE* OF 1912

The four-funnel *France* of 1912 is the natural beginning for a review of twentieth-century French passenger ships. She was the nation's first and only four-stacker, the first large French liner and the beginning of successively bigger, grander and often faster French liners. She joined the already existing big liners of Cunard, White Star, Hamburg America and North German Lloyd; she was France's very first 'floating palace'.

When the keel was laid, on 20 April 1909, for the new flagship of the French Line Compagnie Generale Transatlantique, it was a significant step forward. The new vessel was to be more than twice the size of any previous French passenger ship. Following in the wake of the 11,100-ton sisters *La Lorraine* and *La Savoie* in 1900, and then the 13,700-ton *La Provence* of 1905, it had been intended to call her *La Picardie*. But by the time her launching approached, on 20 September 1911, the name *France* seemed far more appropriate, nationalistic and triumphant. Considerable press attention was focused on the ship, not only for her size but also for her being constructed in a French shipyard, the Penhoet Shipyards at St Nazaire. She was created in a maritime era of high pitch and serious competition. Across the Channel, White Star Line was building the 45,000-ton sisters *Olympic* and *Titanic*, to be followed by the 48,000-ton *Gigantic* (later renamed *Britannic*). Cunard was not left behind – they were planning their 45,000-ton *Aquitania*. But it was the Germans who pulled out all the stops, with a trio of the biggest liners yet created: the 52,000-ton *Imperator*, the 54,000-ton *Vaterland* and finally the 56,000-ton *Bismarck*. Somehow, somewhere, the 23,000-ton *France* would find her place while proudly flying the Tricolour.

The new flagship was France's first turbine-driven passenger liner and also one which had a unique, added feature: an auxiliary engine room abaft of the main engine room. With a foursome of four-bladed propellers that were each very nearly 13ft in diameter, she was intended to do as much as 25 knots at sea. This compared quite favourably against the 21 knots planned for the equally new but larger *Titanic* and slightly surpassed the speed for the much larger *Imperator*. The coal bunkers on the French flagship had a capacity of 5,045 tons, allowing for a daily consumption of approximately 700 tons.

The 713ft-long *France* departed from Le Havre on her maiden crossing to New York on 20 April 1912, a mere five days following the tragic sinking of the *Titanic*. The French were more than grateful that the thoughtful design of their new flagship included a sufficient number of lifeboats.

The four-funnel *France* fitting out at St Nazaire. (Albert Wilhelmi Collection)

161 LE HAVRE. — Le Transatlantique « France » en cale sèche. Vue prise par l'arrière. — LL.

An imposing sight. While in dry dock, the stern of the 23,000-ton *France*, then the largest of all French ships. (Albert Wilhelmi Collection)

The *France* settled in very quickly on the transatlantic circuit, and was favoured not only for her superb decor in first class but also her magnificent cuisine. She was said to have the best kitchens afloat in those two years just before the start of the First World War. Her first-class quarters were soon much favoured by the top end of the Atlantic social set, those millionaires, tycoons and heiresses who ferried to and from Europe on a regular basis, often several times a year. Below decks, her westbound crossings were often heavily booked, filling the 800 berths in steerage. Although there were some teething problems, including a change of propellers within a year, she was judged to be a highly successful ship. The French Line was much encouraged and soon agreed to a contract with the French government for at least four larger liners for passenger and mail service. Bigger still, the 34,000-ton *Paris* was launched as the first of these new liners in 1916.

When the First World War erupted in the summer of 1914, the *France* was quickly pulled out of service and laid up for safety at Brest. The French did not wish to subject their prized flagship to a lurking U-boat. However, her value as an Allied troopship was soon fully realised and so she was transferred to the French government, renamed *France IV* and sent off with troops to the Dardanelles. A year later, in 1915, she was taken to a Toulon shipyard and converted to a hospital ship. This included a complete exterior repainting: white hull colouring, a bold red stripe and Red Cross markings. Over the next two years, she handled thousands of wounded soldiers. She returned to Toulon in 1917 and was refitted as a troopship, carrying mostly American soldiers on eastbound voyages to the trenches of western Europe. When the war ended in November 1918, she had the reverse duty – carrying servicemen home to often enthusiastic welcomes in New York Harbor. She resumed a kind of post-war, austerity passenger service between Brest and New York in January 1919. That summer, in August, sailings were switched to Le Havre. French Line's transatlantic service was, in ways, officially reopened.

The *France*'s enviable reputation was reaffirmed during the heady times of the 1920s. Her lavish interiors prompted her to be dubbed as the 'Chateau of the Atlantic'. She was extensively refitted at St Nazaire between October 1923 and May 1924. Keeping up with the times and change, she was converted from coal to oil fuel and had her interiors modernised. In view of new American immigration quotas, her steerage capacity was cut from 800 to 152. By 1924, her accommodations were for 517 in first class, 444 in second class, 510 in third class and 152 in steerage. She retained a loyal following, even with her reputation as one of the Atlantic's most notorious rollers at sea.

Dubbed the 'Chateau of the Atlantic' for her splendid
decor, this view shows the magnificent, two-deck-high
dining salon. (Albert Wilhelmi Collection)

More splendour at sea. The magnificent Salon XIV
aboard the *France*. (Albert Wilhelmi Collection)

Ocean-going exotica. For 'a breath of the Orient', as French Line advertising noted, here is the Moorish Room, a prized first-class amenity. (Albert Wilhelmi Collection)

Some misfortune struck on 16 June 1928, when the *France* hit a wreck in the Hudson River, New York. Her propellers were seriously damaged. Repairs were made quickly, however, but her future began to fall under more serious review by French Line directors. She was now in third place, following the highly popular *Paris* and the brand-new, decoratively different *Île de France*. The *France*, with her four funnels and period decor, seemed dated and so she was more often shifted to cruising – to the West Indies, the Mediterranean and on summer trips to the Norwegian fjords. When the Depression took hold in the early 1930s, passenger numbers on transatlantic sailings dropped considerably (by 50 per cent between 1930 and 1935) and so cruising became a more viable alternative. The *France* remained popular, often with as many as 200 millionaires on board, lazily moving from port to port. Her kitchens were still excellent, of course, and the decor likened to an old, well-loved hotel.

The aged *France* was, rather expectedly, the first major casualty of the Depression at the French Line. Following the arrival of the medium-sized *Lafayette* (1930) and then the *Champlain* (1932), the old liner was decommissioned in August 1932. She was laid up at Le Havre, 'until better times' according to the Paris headquarters. Idle ships are very vulnerable, however. There was a fire on board the following year, reducing the chances of the 21-year-old ship being revived. With the Atlantic in a worsening slump, the 23,000-ton *France* was sold, in December 1934, to shipbreakers at Dunkirk. She left Le Havre under tow on 15 April 1935. This was just weeks before the maiden sailing of the newest French flagship, the 79,000-ton *Normandie*. What a progression, in little more than twenty years!

2

GRANDEUR AT SEA: THE *PARIS*

She was one of the most popular and best-decorated liners ever to sail the North Atlantic. She was a 'between the wars' liner, finished at the end of more staggering conflict and then destroyed just before the start of a second. She was, quite simply, a ship of enormous style and I can still recall a very evocative photograph of her. It was a highly charismatic scene, so obviously from the stylised 1930s. The wood planking of the ship's decks was heavily shadowed, probably from the late morning sunlight. A heavily veiled, fur-wrapped, designer-dressed Marlene Dietrich sat amidst at least a dozen steamer trunks and cases, all of them smartly dabbed with labels from the French Line, other steamer companies and, of course, the grandest of hotels. The Savoy in London and the Ritz in Paris come to mind. That single photo, run in a glossy retrospective issue of *Vogue*, spoke almost in itself of the high glamour of the great liners and the transatlantic run in its pre-war heyday. The setting was an aft deck on board the *Paris* and Miss Dietrich was heading off for a long vacation in Europe. Regrettably, these days this fine ship – while the first of a masterful five-ship plan sponsored by the French Government – has been largely forgotten. It would seem that her memory has been overshadowed by the likes of three other French liners: the *Île de France*, the *Normandie*, and the much-cherished *France*.

The 34,500grt *Paris* was an immediate follow-up to the high success (and rave reviews) of the 23,600-ton *France* of 1912. The French had, with that mighty four-stacker, entered the large luxury ship class. Indeed, they wanted more – and progressively bigger and better. Their concept was fed by lucrative construction loans and operating subsidies supplied by benevolent ministers at the Ministry of Marine in Paris. Accordingly, at least four big liners were needed to maintain a high-speed, deluxe service to and from New York. While passenger service was certainly an important consideration, the efficient and prompt delivery of mail was equally as such in those pre-aircraft days. The designs and plans for the beautifully appointed *France* were taken out, reworked and enhanced by the Penhoet Shipyards at St Nazaire. The refinements and alterations included a larger ship with three instead of four funnels and a decorative tone that would reach forward rather than backward. It was said the gilded Louis XIV of the earlier liner would seem Art Nouveau, even primitive Art Deco, on the new, 764ft-long vessel.

According to initial plans, the *Paris* would enter service in 1915 and then be followed by two additional, slightly larger liners by 1920. But the outbreak of the First World War in August 1914 changed just about everything – including the commissioning date for the 22-knot *Paris*. While her construction began in 1913, all work stopped in that fateful summer of 1914 and the unfinished hull sat for nearly two years. Then, with special orders from the French government, she was quietly and unceremoniously launched in September 1916. Clearly, the slipway that she occupied was needed for more urgent military craft. The hull of the unfinished liner was towed off to Quiberon and laid up for the duration of the war. At best, French Line plans had to be altered considerably – the *Paris* would be delivered in 1921, the third ship (*Île de France*) moved to 1927 and the fourth (*Lafayette*) to 1930.

The *Paris* was returned to her builder's yard and then completed in 1919–20. After a series of successful sea trials, she was handed over in June 1921 and immediately garnered glowing praises for 'new generation' interiors. She was now ready for a gala, six-night maiden crossing to New York. Based at Le Havre, she called at Southampton, usually tendering while anchored in the Solent, in both directions. There was a very festive reception at New York's Chelsea Piers, the French Line terminal being at Pier 57, conveniently located at the foot of West 15th Street. She immediately became the highly popular flagship of the entire French merchant marine and, to publicists' as well as accountants' delight, the single most popular liner on the Atlantic for much of the 1920s. She had high style, gorgeous interiors, superb service and, of course, more of French Line's magnificent cooking.

In A.G. Norton's *Ships of the North Atlantic*, published in London in 1936, he wrote much about the glorious *Paris*:

For the greater part, this ship is very modern, but in some of the rooms, the earlier styles persist, although all of them have very modern fittings. The cabins are very well arranged and ten of suites have private verandas. The Sun Deck has the Terrace Cafe, part of which is open to the outdoor deck, and forward of the Cafe is the Balcony of the Smoking Room from which stairs lead down to the Main Smoking Room on the Promenade Deck with its modern furniture and indirect lighting.

The Promenade Deck is enclosed with glass screens for the whole of its length and is brought out slightly on each side. It is also rubber-tiled to deaden sound and to prevent slipping. Other rooms on this deck beside the Main Smoking Room are the 'Salon de The', where 'moderne' is the style and which is supplemented by light-colored walls, indirect lighting and a large skylight. In the centre of this room is one of the finest achievements of the decorators of the *Paris*, namely an illuminated dance floor, where frosted glass panels in

Pier 57, Manhattan was said to be the 'beginning of your trip to France'. The *France* is on the left, the larger *Paris* on the right. (Author's Collection)

the actual floor are illuminated from beneath by lights, giving a very pleasing effect. Next is the Balcony of the Main Foyer. Then, there's the Grand Salon in the style of Marie Antoinette yet in a modern way. It has a large dome, the topmost part of which is glass, as well as large windows and mirrors. At one end is a stage. Forward of this is the panelled library, where books in both French and English can be found. The foremost room on the Promenade Deck is the gymnasium, which is well equipped and well lighted.

Norton's written tour of the *Paris* concluded:

The next deck down is A Deck where the Main Entrance can be found. Here also is the Main Foyer where fine woods are cleverly introduced. Indirect lighting gives an admirable effect and ironwork on the wide stairs is definitely the feature. On C Deck is the Main Dining Room from which a large stairway leads to the Balcony Dining Saloon, supported by square pillars, over which a large glass dome forming a central nave with an aisle on each side, both upstairs and downstairs. Halfway up the staircase at one end of the Dining Saloon is an array of magnificent mirrors reflecting the light and colors of the room. There are 130 tables in the restaurant, most of which seat four persons each.

The *Paris* did have a rather unusual share of mishaps, however. On 15 October 1927, she rammed and sank the freighter *Bessengen* off New York Harbor's Robbins Reef Lighthouse. Six were killed. On 6 April 1929, she went aground, in New York's Lower Bay. Her captain later reported, 'After passing the Statue of Liberty, we encountered heavy fog, with visibility at a half mile or less, and then, quite suddenly, the pilot misjudged.' Less than two weeks later, on 18 April, she was aground once again, this time off England's Eddystone Light. But far more serious problems were ahead. On 20 August, the *Paris* was almost completely destroyed by fire while at her Le Havre berth. The blaze began in the third-class accommodations, spread to second class and then into the first-class quarters. Initial reports suggested that she might have to be scrapped. However, within five months she was repaired, restored and even modernised at her builders at St Nazaire. Her berthing plans were rearranged at the same time – from 563 to 560 in first class, 460 to 530 in second class and 1,092 down to 844 in third class.

The *Paris* was affected by the declining transatlantic passenger demands of the early Depression. In a rather desperate search for alternate revenue, she was sent off on one-class cruises. In the winter of 1931, she departed on her first Mediterranean cruise, to Tenerife, Casablanca, Gibraltar, Algiers, Naples, Corsica, Monte Carlo, Cannes, Majorca and the Azores. Reasonably priced at just over $16 a day, these fares included the option of leaving the ship on the French Riviera and then travelling by train for a stay in Paris, and then to Le Havre for a return to New York on the new *Île de France*. One advertisement for these *Paris* cruises included reference to the otherwise bleak economic times: 'Old General Depression will not be allowed up the gangplank; these cruises are planned to make Time – which all economists say is the cure – really go to work for you!'

When the *Normandie* came into service in the spring of 1935, and as the veteran *France* was sold to the breakers, the 14-year-old *Paris* became the oldest big liner in the French Line fleet. But her requirements on the North Atlantic had declined steadily and she turned more and more to cruising. That same year, there were rumours that she would be converted for full-time cruising and would even be redone with all-white, heat-resistant hull colouring. She was never repainted, however, although one large brochure showed her in this guise. Often leased to the big Raymond-Whitcomb travel firm at New York, one of the very last cruises for the *Paris* was a five-week 'Early Summer' itinerary that departed in June 1938, bound for Madeira, Lisbon, Santander, St Jean-de-Lux, Bordeaux, St Nazaire, Lorient,

The highly popular *Paris* outbound at Le Havre. (Cronican-Arroyo Collection)

A sad ending, fire ravaged the *Paris* at her Le Havre berth on 19 April 1939 and then firefighters' water caused the 763ft-long liner to capsize. Her wreckage remained in this spot for eight years. This viewis dated 25 April 1939. (Cronican-Arroyo Collection)

and they committed an ill common to burning ships: too much firefighting water. A day later, the *Paris* capsized. With less than a quarter of her starboard size poking above the local waters, she was a total loss. Her two masts had to be immediately cut so that the *Normandie* could be moved out of the graving dock. Little else was done to the burned-out *Paris*, however. There were strong hints of sabotage and then far greater worries as the Nazis mounted for war and finally invaded Poland on 1 September. The Second World War started and so salvage of the *Paris* became less and less of a concern.

During the thorough bombings on Le Havre in 1944, the wreckage of the *Paris* was damaged further still. Afterwards, in 1945–46 and with the war's end, clearing harbour debris and repairing damaged docks and terminals were foremost concerns. Again, the *Paris* was left

Brest, Cobh, Dublin, Greenock, Oslo, Gothenburg, Copenhagen and then Le Havre. Fares included return to New York on any of the other French liners. Full passage rates began at $550 (£110).

The beautiful *Paris* was also a femme fatale. While being loaded with art treasures bound for exhibition at the New York World's Fair of 1939–40, she became yet another victim of fire, that vulnerability so common to French and French-built ships. The blaze broke out on 19 April 1939 as the ship was berthed at Le Havre, with the *Champlain* just ahead and the *Normandie* behind in the huge graving dock. Firefighters were immediately summoned,

untouched. There was still time for one more incident involving the former liner. In December 1946, when the former German super liner *Europa* was about to begin her refit and makeover as the French *Liberté*, she was ripped from her moorings by a fierce Atlantic gale and slammed into the wreckage of the *Paris*. Fortunately, while the *Liberté* was holed badly, she settled in an upright position for the most part and therefore could be salvaged and repaired. As for the last remains of the *Paris*, authorities at Le Havre finally realised that her sunken remains were a menace. She was dismantled where she lay during 1947.

3

A LONG AND VARIED LIFE: THE *DE GRASSE*

A teacher of mine went to Europe in 1950. It was all very exciting, even glamorous. A whole summer in Europe! She crossed on the *De Grasse* and, while that smaller ship was hardly say the *Normandie* or the *Île de France*, it was very special. She often spoke of the sheer glamour, style and certainly the 'magnificent food from morning until midnight' on board the French liner. To her, the *De Grasse* might have been a grand super liner – it was her special ship. She returned to New York aboard the *Queen Mary*, also in tourist class, but she rather oddly had very little to say about that Cunarder. The *De Grasse* was the standout in her recollections of that joyous summer.

The French Line, the Compagnie Generale Transatlantique (CGT) is perhaps best remembered for its large, finely run, magnificently fed, big ocean liners – ships such as the *Paris*, *Île de France* and *Normandie*. There were also any number of intermediate, smaller-sized and less grand passenger ships. One of the finest and long-lived of this group was the 17,700grt *De Grasse*. Completed in 1924, she was used for many years on the otherwise prestigious run to New York.

Ordered from British builders, the Cammell Laird yard at Birkenhead, near Liverpool, her first keel plates were actually laid in March 1920. She was a post-First World War replacement and to be called *Suffren*, but delays and material shortages meant her launching did not take place for almost four years, not until February 1924. By then, however, there had been some changes, including the decision to rename the ship *De Grasse*. Afterwards, there was still another complication: a long strike at the Cammell Laird yard. Now impatient, the French had the nearly complete ship moved to St Nazaire for final fitting-out and completion. Finally, in the summer of 1924, the 574ft-long *De Grasse* set off on a maiden voyage to New York.

The 16-knot *De Grasse* was designed with quarters for 399 cabin class and as many as 1,712 third-class passengers. She supplemented the larger *France*, *Paris* and later *Île de France* on the New York service, but occasionally was sent, during the slack winter season, on cruises to the Caribbean or on the colonial liner route to Guadeloupe and Martinique, as well as other Caribbean ports.

She made headline news in November 1929. The *New York Times* reported:

The French liner *De Grasse* … steamed slowly down the Hudson yesterday morning [9 November], was caught by a strong ebb tide and swung against the freighter *Pequonnack* and Pier 14 at the foot of Fulton Street. The bow of the freighter was smashed and the pier damaged, but no one was injured. The French ship itself was not damaged. This is the second incident in which French Line ships have been involved in a month. The *Paris* rammed and sank the Norwegian freighter *Bessengen* off the Statue of Liberty the night of 15 October.

Troubled times. Already repainted in wartime greys, the *De Grasse* is seen at Halifax harbor in a view dated autumn 1939. (Cronican-Arroyo Collection)

In the increasing decline caused by the Depression, the *De Grasse* was refitted and upgraded in 1932 so as to be more suitable for cruising. There were also periods of idleness with the ship being laid up. There seemed to be little place for the *De Grasse*, especially after the debut of the exquisite *Normandie* in the spring of 1935. There were reports that she was to be refitted for a new South Pacific service, connecting Tahiti with Australia and New Zealand and perhaps even the American West Coast. This never came about. Instead, she was refitted and then operated by New York-based Simmons Tours for a series of sunshine trips in southern waters – nine days to Nassau and Havana, and with fares starting at $100 (£20). There were also special calls at Miami, then rather unusual for New York-based cruise liners. On Saturday morning in February 1939, the *De Grasse* was included in one of the greatest gatherings of ocean liners at pre-war New York. Others included the *Hamburg*, *Bremen*, *Columbus*, *Normandie*, *Britannic*, *Aquitania*, *Conte di Savoia* and *Monarch of Bermuda*.

Rebuilt with a single funnel after the Second World War, the modernised *De Grasse* departs from Le Havre in this view dated 1948. United States Lines' *Washington* is berthed to the left. (Albert Wilhelmi Collection)

Later that same year, in October, and after the start of the Second World War, the *De Grasse* was among the first liners to safely deliver evacuees to still-neutral America, including fleeing European Jews. She eventually returned to Le Havre and, under orders from the French government, was sent to Bordeaux for lay-up and safety. Her future was uncertain. Unfortunately, she later fell into Nazi hands and was used by them as a military accommodation ship, but without ever leaving her moorings. In their retreat, on 30 August 1944, the Nazis sank the liner. She was salvaged exactly a year to the day, on 30 August 1945, and brought to St Nazaire for restoration. The French Line was much depleted; only two liners remained, the other being the *Île de France* (which remained in military service until 1947). Two years later, in July 1947, streamlined with a single, wide funnel and modified with quarters for 500 in cabin class and 470 in tourist class, the flag-bedecked *De Grasse* reopened French Line's luxury service to New York. Her companions at the time were two passenger-freighters: the *Oregon*, accommodating seventy-five passengers, and the *Wisconsin*, with fifty-seven berths.

In her first two seasons, 1947 and 1948, the *De Grasse* was almost fully booked on every sailing. The arrival of the brilliant *Île de France*, first planned to be built in 1948, was delayed and finally rescheduled for the summer of 1949. The addition of the *Liberté*, the former German *Europa*, seemed further off, even remote. She was not added to the French Line schedules until August 1950.

In 1952, the *De Grasse* was replaced on the New York run by the new *Flandre* and so was moved full time to the Le Havre–West Indies run, sailing in company with another pre-war liner, the *Colombie* of 1931. It was all a short-lived change, however. A year later, she was replaced by the brand-new *Antilles* and then, rather hurriedly, was bought by Canadian Pacific Steamships, which were in rather desperate need of replacement tonnage for their *Empress of Canada*, which had burned out and capsized at her Liverpool berth in January 1953. There was a great demand for Atlantic passages, especially for the coronation in London of Queen Elizabeth II that June. The *De Grasse* was the ideal replacement. In quick time, the French Tricolour was lowered, the British Red Ensign hoisted, and the ship itself renamed *Empress of Australia*.

In October 1955, after three good seasons on the Liverpool–Montreal run, she was again replaced (by the brand-new *Empress of Britain*) and was again for sale. But again, and in rather quick time, she found new owners, this time under the Italian flag. She was formally transferred, in February 1956, to the Grimaldi-Siosa Lines, who were then actively engaged in the Caribbean migrant trades. Renamed *Venezuela*, she was assigned to a mid-Atlantic service – outwards from Naples, Genoa, Cannes, Barcelona and Tenerife to

Commerce on the docks. The *De Grasse* is loading along the Le Havre dockside for a crossing to New York, with the *Washington* just behind. (Albert Wilhelmi Collection)

Guadeloupe, Martinique, La Guaira and Trinidad. She proved very popular and was Siosa's largest and possibly finest ship. In 1960, she underwent an extensive, life-extending rebuilding wherein a new flair bow was fitted (increasing her overall length to 614ft) and her capacity enlarged to 1,480 – 180 first class, 500 tourist class and 800 third-class passengers.

Unfortunately, while she might have continued for some years (perhaps to her fiftieth year), she stranded on rocks near Cannes on 17 March 1962. Her passengers and crew were taken ashore and all of the ship's future sailings cancelled. Once refloated, hull examinations revealed major damages that would require long, expensive repairs. Her advanced age was also against her. That summer, she was sold to Italian shipbreakers and towed to La Spezia for demolition. It was the end for one of the most enduring of all French passenger ships.

Another ship used in the French West Indies trade was the 13,300grt *Colombie*, completed in 1931. She was in many ways a miniature version of the *Île de France*, *Lafayette* and forthcoming *Champlain*. Her accommodations included a descending stairwell into her first-class restaurant, a noted and very popular French Line feature, and other decorative touches that reflected the glories of Art Deco at sea.

Used by the Americans during the Second World War, first as a trooper and then as the specially outfitted hospital ship the USS *Aleda E. Lutz*, the

Changing hats. In the third and last career of her long life, the former *De Grasse* is seen at Lisbon as the Italian-flag *Venezuela*. (Roger Scozzafava Collection)

509ft-long ship was not returned, despite pressing post-war needs, to French commercial service until as late as October 1950. After the war, she continued to serve as a hospital ship, but out in troubled French Indochina. Afterwards, she underwent a very extensive, two-year rebuilding at Flushing in Holland. Her place on the mid-Atlantic run to the West Indies was temporarily filled by the 9,400grt *Katoomba*, a passenger ship chartered from the Greek Line. Built in 1913 for the Australian coastal run, she was quite unique, even in the late 1940s, because she still burned coal for fuel.

When the *Colombie* resumed her liner sailings, she had a more contemporary passenger arrangement for 192 in first class, 140 in cabin class and 246 in tourist class, and was topped by a new, single, tapered funnel (replacing the original twin stacks). She was routed from Le Havre and Southampton to Pointe-a-Pitre, Roseau, Fort de France, St Lucia, Trinidad, Barbados, Fort de France and then Pointe-a-Pitre before returning to Le Havre via Plymouth. Cargo and government-subsidised mails were, of course, an important part of her economics. She was very popular with passengers, both one-way traffic to and from the Caribbean as well as round-trip travellers who often came aboard in the European winter season.

The late John Havers, a noted ship historian at the port of Southampton, had recollections of this smaller French liner:

In the late 1930s, I visited the *Colombie* by tender off Cowes. She was almost a miniature *Normandie* with bright, colorful public rooms. Then she carried some 200 passengers in first class and her special feature was advertised as a particularly efficient Punkah-Louvre (forced air) ventilation system, supplemented by constructional aids for added cooling. The first class dining room had sliding doors in the ship's sides, giving direct access to the sea air and leaving just a protective grill. Thus, the speed of the ship gave a constant breeze direct from the sea to the dining tables. The Grand Salon had folding doors opening directly into the cool Winter Garden. The French certainly did their best in the absence of full air-conditioning for a ship built as far back as 1931. Her two triple-steam whistles made a wonderful whopping blast, a note not heard much nowadays. When bidding farewell from a departing tender, it was a moment not easily forgotten.

The *Colombie* continued on the West Indies run until 1962–63, then was sold off to the Greek-flag Typaldos Lines to become the *Atlantica* and was used mostly in the Mediterranean. Typaldos collapsed into bankruptcy in 1967 and ships such as the *Atlantica* were seized, laid up, and later auctioned off for scrapping (she was partly demolished in Greece in 1970 and then towed to Spain and finished off four years later).

4

DECORATIVE INNOVATOR:
THE STUNNING *ÎLE DE FRANCE*

When the celebrated *Paris* first appeared in 1921, she was, in so many ways, merely a grand hint of the French Line's next transatlantic ship 'dreamboat', the 43,100grt *Île de France*, which was commissioned in the spring of 1927. She was one of the most important liners of the twentieth century. Her degree of fresh, new modernity as well as innovative style were unlike anything previously seen, not only on the Atlantic, but anywhere. In Time-Life's *The Great Liners*, the *Île* – as she was often fondly called – was described as having 'a special verve; she was the Jazz Age flapper of flappers. With her 29ft-long bar – where Americans could flout Prohibition, drinking Scotch at 15 cents a glass – and her sidewalk cafe, the *Île de France* signaled what a lot of the world wanted to hear after the war and the fatigue and doubt of the early twenties: "The old days are back. Let the good times roll"'.

Time-Life wrote more about the 791ft-long *Île*, rather typically built at St Nazaire:

Like every French Line ship that had gone before her, the *Île de France* was lavish in decor. With 40 columns soaring in her main lounge, she evoked an elegant Classicism; with her varnished wood veneer discreetly sheathing steel underpinnings, she was modern without being vulgar. A hefty share of the 1920s ocean-going public found that the *Île* was an agreeable modish place to sit out an ocean crossing, a fact evident from the quarter of a million passengers who made 347 crossings on her in the next twelve years [until the Second World War started in September 1939].

John Malcolm Brinnin, in his excellent *The Sway of the Grand Saloon*, wrote:

Designed by more than 30 different French firms, the *Île de France* managed to absorb and integrate all influences. Her 'tremendous' main dining room was 20ft wider than the Church of the Madeleine; the dance floor in the Salon de Conversation measured 516 sq.ft; the bar in the first class lounge was the 'longest afloat'. Where other ships had conventional garden lounges, she had a complete Parisian sidewalk cafe with awnings above, and saucers marked '6 francs' on tables; in her children's playroom, there was a real carousel with painted ponies and proper music to go round by.

Wishing to show all the richness and all the imagination of French decorative art, the French Line decided to make the 439 cabins in first class different from each other and to add four apartments of great luxury and ten of luxury … Furthermore, the ship was decorated with statues by Baudry and Dejean, bas reliefs by Jeanniot, Bouchard and Saupique, enamel panels by Schmied, artistic ironwork by Subes and Szabo, paintings by Ducos de la Haille, Gernez, Balandre, and not forgetting the chapel, an admirable Stations of the Cross sculptured in wood by Le Bourgeois.

Passengers on board the *Île de France*, especially in first class, enjoyed a new, sleek luxury. The great first-class dining room, for example, towered three decks in height. Never before had the travelling public seen a room of such massive simplicity yet startling attractiveness. It was designed as opposed to copied from some landside theme, as all of the earlier liners had used; it was created for the ship itself in originality. The era of 'ocean liner style' had begun, originated by the French, and would lead to some of the largest and grandest liners of all time, such as the *Normandie* in 1935. Long before completion, that great ship was commonly referred to as the 'super *Île de France*'.

Tense times. The *Île de France* departs from Pier 88, New York, in late August 1939. It would be the final eastbound crossing for the French liner for almost seven years. (Cronican-Arroyo Collection).

The end of the war. In late 1945, while repainted with French Line funnel colours, the *Île de France* arrives at Halifax with returning troops. (Halifax Maritime Museum)

A modern Greek temple. The magnificent first-class dining salon aboard the *Île de France* in high Art Deco styling. (Richard Faber Collection)

A gala occasion. The handsome motorliner *Lafayette* arrives in New York Harbor for the first time. White Star's *Adriatic* is seen on the far left. (Albert Wilhelmi Collection)

Fleetmates. The outbound *Lafayette* departs just in front of the *Colombie*. (Albert Wilhelmi Collection)

More splendour on the seas: The glorious music room aboard the *Lafayette*. (Albert Wilhelmi Collection)

Dressed in flags for her maiden voyage, the *Champlain* casts off from Bordeaux before sailing to Le Havre and then across to New York. (Albert Wilhelmi Collection)

Summer cruising. The *Lafayette* on a cruise from Le Havre to the Norwegian fjords and rather remote Spitzbergen. (Albert Wilhelmi Collection)

Caribbean bound. The *Colombie* departs from Bordeaux en route to the sunny isles of the West Indies. (Albert Wilhelmi Collection)

The modern-looking *Champlain* at St Nazaire, 1932. (Albert Wilhelmi Collection).

A new look: Just as Paris fashions change, the *Colombie* was rebuilt in 1948–50 and, among other changes, fitted with a single, tapered funnel. (Albert Wilhelmi Collection)

Mediterranean waters: By the mid-1930s, the 10,000grt *Ville d'Alger* and her sister, the *Ville d'Oran*, were the biggest liners in French service between Marseilles and North Africa. (Albert Wilhelmi Collection)

5

UGLY DUCKLING TO SWAN: THE *FELIX ROUSSEL*

Time to talk of the colonies, the other French passenger ship runs, away from the prestigious, but so often documented, North Atlantic route.

In the darkness of a summer's night in 1972, I recall sailing from Amsterdam (aboard the cruise ship *Regina Magna*, the former *Pasteur* of 1939 and documented within these pages), on a Northern cruise, to the Baltic capitals and London. As we passed IJmuiden, I noticed the largely unlit silhouette of a moored passenger liner. Quickly, I realised it was the former *Arosa Sun*, which had been the French *Felix Roussel* in her previous

life. Indeed, an unusual ship, it was very interesting to see her. I remembered her from her visits to New York in the late 1950s, sailing for the otherwise short-lived Arosa Line.

France's Messageries Maritimes, whose ships had been trading out to the Far East since 1862, astonished the marine design world in the late 1920s with a series of passenger ships that had, according to at least one maritime journal, 'freak appearances'. These ships were fitted with sets of square – yes, square – stacks. They were short in height, broad-rimmed at the top and

An eccentric design. Messageries Maritimes' *Jean La Borde,* photographed early in the war on 16 January 1940, with her very unusual square funnels. (Author's Collection)

painted entirely in black or white, according to the period. No one dared to claim that these were 'pretty paquebots'. One of these ships was the 16,700grt *Felix Roussel*, named for a past president of Messageries Maritimes. She was launched in December 1929.

Built by Ateliers et Chantiers de la Loire at St Nazaire and completed in the autumn of 1930, the 568ft-long ship immediately joined what was then a vital and steady link out to the 'Extreme Orient' – from Marseilles via Port Said and the Suez Canal to Djibouti, Colombo, Singapore, Saigon (then a major French colonial outpost), Hong Kong, Shanghai and turnaround at Kobe. On some voyages there were added stopovers at Madras, Rangoon, Bangkok, Haiphong, Manila and Yokohama. *The Felix Roussel* sailed in company with such other Messageries Maritimes liners as the *Porthos, Aramis, President Doumer, Jean La Borde* and *Athos II*. For the twenty-three-day voyage from Marseilles to Saigon, the first-class fare in the late 1930s was priced from $420 (£80) and third class was from $190 (£40).

The diesel-driven *Felix Roussel* could also carry lots of freight (especially large quantities of mail and those diplomatic bags, and often returned with Asian silks and spices) along with her 398 passengers – 196 in first class, 113 in second class and 89 in third. On board, there were the colonial high commissioners and their entourages as well as rich traders, tourists,

Family gathering. Four Messageries Maritimes passenger ships are together at Marseilles – from left to right are the *Viet-Nam, Laos, Felix Roussel* and *Marechal Joffre*. (Richard Faber Collection)

A changed appearance. After the Second World War, the *Felix Roussel* was rebuilt with a single, more traditional funnel. (Albert Wilhelmi Collection)

More squared funnels. The 10,000grt *Eridan*, built in 1928, had the unusual look of square stacks as well. Belonging to Messageries Maritimes, she was used on the Marseilles–Suez–Far East run. (Author's Collection)

For Paquet Lines' service from Marseilles to West Africa, the fleet was headed, in the 1930s, by the 8,800-grt sisters *Koutoubia* (seen here at Marseilles) and the *Djenne*. (Albert Wilhelmi Collection)

Speedy crossing to North Africa. One of the fastest ships on the Marseilles-Algeria run in the 1930s was the squat-stack, motor liner *El Kantara*, operated by Compagnie de Navigation Mixte. (Author's Collection)

Stately ships. Dating from 1912, Fabre Line operated the three-funnel *Providence* and her sister *Patria* on the Marseilles–East Mediterranean run. (Author's Collection)

the French colonial police, the soldiers, civil servants, artisans and migrants. Young Asians used her for trips for schooling in 'Mother France'.

Used as an Allied trooper during the war (she was seized at Port Said in the summer of 1940, soon after the fall of France), she was returned to the French, to Messageries Maritimes, in 1947 and then underwent a thorough refit and modernisation at a Dunkirk shipyard in 1948–50. Rather sensibly, her owners took the opportunity to remove those offending square funnels and in their place substituted one large, normal-shaped, raked one. Overall, it made her a more elegant-looking ship. She was called a 'white swan' in Company literature.

Her interior decor remained much the same, however. The basic theme had come from the Khmer period. A special booklet was issued to reacquaint the travelling public with the ship's 'Oriental magnificence'. The 15-knot *Felix Roussel* was a floating treasury of elaborate carving, panelling and beautiful woodwork. Some thought it a trifle overpowering, especially by the 1950s, a little too big and even slightly ecclesiastical. The first-class dining room, for example, was reached down a broad stairwell with two balustrades beautifully carved and depicting the forms of two Negas, whose seven heads outspread at the bottom of the stairwell in the shape of an open fan. The centre of the dining room represented one of the open courtyards of Angkor Wat. The ceiling was painted in blue and illuminated by special lights concealed in a modern Cambodian vase. The impression was one of the sky

above. It was all intended to entice passengers to linger longer over good food and fine wine. Incidentally, the catering on Messageries Maritimes passenger ships was contracted out to a firm used by them for years.

The Salon de Musique was notable for its octagonal dome, surrounded by an illuminated fresco depicting danseurs and danseuses. The chairs were covered in gold silk. The cabins in first class were all very comfortable, spacious and well fitted out. A special feature of her cabin deluxe was a circular table of adjustable height that could be used for private dining. In all, the *Felix Roussel* was a popular ship, even into the '50s, blending the French way of living with the splendours of an Oriental setting.

The liner service to increasingly troubled French Indo-China began to change. The old trade quickly fell away and so Messageries Maritimes began to retire their older ships. In 1955, the *Felix Roussel* was sold to the Swiss-owned Arosa Line, hoisted the Panamanian flag and became their *Arosa Sun*. Restyled with sixty berths in a small, intimate first class and nearly 900 in tourist, she was put on transatlantic service, mostly between Northern Europe and Eastern Canada. She also did some winter, off-season cruising from New York. In December 1958, when Arosa collapsed into bankruptcy, she was impounded for debts at Bremerhaven and fell into the hands of a Swiss bank. She was later sold off to a Dutch steelmaker and moved, in September 1960, to IJmuiden to become a stationary workers' accommodation ship. She remained there until 1974, when she was towed to Spain for scrapping.

Another life. The French *Campana*, used on the Marseilles–South American run, became the Italian *Irpinia* in 1955. She is seen here at Plymouth, preparing for a voyage to the West Indies. (Richard Faber Collection)

Another ex-Frenchman. Sailing in the '50s and '60s, the Italian *Ascania* had been the French *Florida*, dating from 1926. (Alex Duncan)

6

QUEEN OF THE SOUTH ATLANTIC: *L'ATLANTIQUE*

Europe–South America services flourished in the 1920s and '30s. Routes to the East Coast of South America – to Brazil, Uruguay and Argentina – were especially popular. There was the regular trade in first and second classes of government officials, business people, rich travellers and even the occasional tourist, but third class, particularly on the southbound sailings, had a special clientele – great numbers of Europeans seeking new lives, with greater social and economic opportunities in Latin America. Others were escaping the harsh times of the Depression of the 1930s. The Germans, Dutch, British, Spanish, Portuguese and Italians each had passenger ships employed on the southern run to Rio de Janeiro, Santos, Montevideo and Buenos Aires. The service was capped around 1930 by the 27,500grt *Cap Arcona* of Germany's Hamburg–South America Line, the 22,000grt sisters *Alcantara* and *Asturias* of Britain's Royal Mail Lines and, biggest of all, the 32,500grt near-sisters *Roma* and *Augustus* of Italy's soon-to-be-amalgamated Italian Line. Certainly, the French, namely the Compagnie de Navigation Sud-Atlantique, were not to be left out. They planned a large, lavish liner, a ship described as a 'first cousin of the *Île de France*'.

Fitting out. The splendid but ill-fated *L'Atlantique* fitting out at St Nazaire in 1931. (Albert Wilhelmi Collection)

The large, very grand, decoratively stunning *L'Atlantique* might have been the biggest liner yet for South American service, but she also had the shortest life. She sailed for only sixteen months – from September 1931 until January 1933.

Built at the Penhoet Shipyards at St Nazaire, where the *France*, *Paris* and *Île de France* had been constructed, the 742ft-long *L'Atlantique* was ceremoniously launched on 15 April 1930. Certainly an exciting liner, she would be completed at a tender time – the beginning of the worldwide Depression. From the start, her owners were not expecting high passenger loads or huge profits. She was commissioned in the autumn of 1931 and promptly set off on her maiden voyage, from Bordeaux to Rio de Janeiro, Santos, Montevideo and Buenos Aires. She was highly praised from the start for her luxuries, the lavish and spacious on-board feel, and the high level (following the *Île de France*) of Art Deco styling. At 42,512 gross tons, she carried 414 first-class, 158 second-class and 584 third-class passengers. She ranked as the twelfth-largest liner afloat.

She had one noted blemish, however. In the beginning, her short, almost squat, funnels spoiled her appearance – she looked top heavy, almost clumsy, certainly far from beautiful. Promptly, her three funnels were raised in height and the effect was a much more pleasing exterior.

But, on 4 January 1933, while on a 'positioning voyage' without passengers between Bordeaux and Le Havre, where she was to have her winter overhaul in the big graving dock there, a fire started in a first-class cabin. It spread to the electric conduits. In less than three hours the liner was ablaze from end to end. Orders were given to abandon ship. There was more misfortune. One of the first lifeboats to be lowered fell into the sea when the davit ropes snapped. Seven or eight seamen were thrown into the English Channel waters and drowned. Some crew members stayed in the engine room too long and were killed, while others were trapped and killed by the fast-moving flames. There followed reports of the deaths of several waiters, who had secretly boarded in Bordeaux for a 'free ride' to Le Havre.

High luxury on the high seas. The bedroom of an apartment de luxe aboard the 42,000grt *L'Atlantique*. (Richard Faber Collection)

A sad voyage. The fire-ravaged remains of the *L'Atlantique* being towed into Cherbourg, January 1933. (Albert Wilhelmi Collection)

The burnt-out *L'Atlantique* remained at Cherbourg for three years, until 1936. (Author's Collection)

L'Atlantique was completely abandoned the following day. It was drifting and soon took on a 20-degree list to port. The flames had subsided, but great plumes of smoke still wafted upward from the smouldering hulk. She drifted some 25 miles west of the island of Guernsey and tugs were dispatched, but they couldn't get cloe to the ship. Her hull was still 'red hot', as one newspaper reported.

Almost immediately, the fire and total destruction of *L'Atlantique* was compared to another new liner, the *Georges Philippar* of Messageries Maritimes. The *Georges Philippar* was destroyed just months before, in May 1932, while making her return maiden voyage to Marseilles from the Far East. While sailing in the Gulf of Aden, a fire erupted due to defective electrical wiring, which led to an accumulation of high electrical charges throughout the ship's framework. Fires soon broke out all over the 42,500-ton vessel. Immediately, some French newspapers suggested 'electrical problems' on board *L'Atlantique*. Other newspapers were more dramatic – they suggested sabotage.

By 7 January, three days after the fire, nine rescue tugs towed the scorched *L'Atlantique* to Cherbourg. There were doubts that she would survive the tow. Now listing heavily to starboard, she was a powerless mass coping with high winds, waves and currents. Fearing further complications, she was anchored for a time outside Cherbourg Harbour. Once docked, the local fire brigade boarded and put out the last smouldering blaze. The interiors were in total ruins, but there was still hope for the ship. News reports already suggested the $3 million (£600,000) ship might be worth a scant $100,000 (£20,000) in scrap.

In the first months at Cherbourg, insurance underwriters, among others, swarmed over the corpse of the once great liner. Her owners announced that they had no intention of repairing and rebuilding the ship. Three years of wrangling followed. *L'Atlantique* sat quiet and untouched, a monument of sorts to careless ruination. Finally, in 1935, insurance monies amounting to $6.8 million (£1.3 million) were settled in favour of the ship's owner. Soon afterwards, she was sold for scrap, going to the Smith & Houston works at Port Glasgow. While under tow in the spring of 1936, she passed the brand-new *Queen Mary*. Indeed, the two ships presented a great contrast; alone, in the annals of French passenger ship history, the saga of the otherwise beautiful *L'Atlantique* was one of the saddest.

In addition to the *Georges Philippar* and *L'Atlantique*, it can be noted that fire destroyed a good number of other French liners, namely the *Lafayette* in 1938, the *Paris* in 1939, the *Normandie* in 1942 and the *Antilles* in 1971. Even in their 'afterlife', while in later careers for other owners, fires prevailed. This list includes the likes of the *Bianca 'C'* (ex-*La Marseillaise*) in 1961, the former *Viet-Nam/Pacifique* in 1974, the ex-*Laos* in 1976 and the *Pallas Athena* (ex-*Flandre*) in 1994.

7

LA BELLE FRANCE: THE SUMPTUOUS *NORMANDIE*

The *Normandie* was the ultimate transatlantic ocean liner – assuredly of the 1930s, but perhaps of the entire twentieth century. She had abundance – she was innovative, glittering, exceptionally advanced – truly sensational. She was, of course, the result of a successive series of bigger and better French liners, beginning with the *France* of 1912 and continuing to the *Île de France* (1927) and *L'Atlantique* (1931). Even the far smaller *Champlain* (1932) has often been called a prelude. She also drew from existing big Atlantic liners, ships such as the *Bremen, Europa, Empress of Britain, Rex* and *Conte di Savoia*. Her French creators, designers and decorators sought perfection and then, or so it would seem, went one step further.

Her purpose was distinctly threefold: to be the largest liner afloat (the first to exceed 60,000 tons and 1,000ft in length); to be the fastest ship; and, thirdly, to be an extraordinary floating centre of 'everything French' – from food to decor to style and fashion. The French Government was very enthusiastic and subsidised much of the $60 million (£12 million) construction cost, itself then the greatest amount paid for a passenger liner. (Comparatively, the 225,000-ton, 6,400-berth *Allure of the Seas*, the world's largest liner in 2013, cost $1.5 billion (£700 million) when built in Finland in 2010.) In buoyant foresight, her Parisian benefactors and owners realised that only the best possible image for France could result from this great ship. The *Normandie* succeeded in all three intentions and then even went further in terms of her almost extraordinary impact on the world in terms of decoration, dining, films and even children's toys. She was, without question, the most important ship and certainly the greatest and grandest of all French liners.

The first keel plates were laid down at St Nazaire in January 1931, indeed an alternately tense time with the worldwide Depression taking a more serious hold. While many names were suggested, including *Jean D'Arc, La*

Belle France and even *Maurice Chevalier*, she was launched as the *Normandie* on 29 October 1932. The towering but unfinished 28,000-ton hull slipped into the Loire with such a mighty backwash that it swept 100 workers and onlookers into the water. Immediately, she was linked to a sense of drama – the beautiful woman who could not find complete happiness. Much of France itself was full of excitement and anticipation. Newspapers, magazines and cinema newsreels often reported on the new ship. There was, however, considerable unemployment and food and bread lines across the nation by 1932. Consequently, not every Frenchman was flushed with pride when thinking of this extravagant liner, its exceptional cost and the idea that she was actually created more for the Americans, especially rich Americans.

The *Normandie* entered service in the spring of 1935, to great success, gala receptions and welcomes, and with further triumph at winning the prized

Preparation. The splendid *Normandie* prepares to leave St Nazaire for sea trials. (Author's Collection)

Longer than the Hall of Mirrors at Versailles, the magnificent first-class dining room on board the *Normandie*. It was done in bronze, hammered glass and Lalique. (Albert Wilhelmi Collection)

Blue Riband for speed. With a record of 29.98 knots, she beat out the previous winner, Italy's *Rex* and her speed of 28.92 knots.

The interested public, especially at New York it seems, marvelled at her contemporary, even advanced, raked silhouette of three funnels, each diminishing in height moving aft. Her outdoor decks were meticulously cleared – there was not a ventilator, deckhouse or chain locker out of place. Everything was thoughtfully hidden below. The bow was finely raked. But if her exterior appearance was striking, the interiors were the true masterpiece.

The *Normandie* – carrying 1,972 passengers (848 in first class, 670 in tourist and 454 in third) – was certainly the most extravagantly decorated liner of her day, perhaps of all time. The main dining room, for example, was done in hammered glass, bronze and Lalique, and was slightly longer than the Hall of Mirrors at Versailles. It rose three decks in height. The theatre was the first ever fitted to a liner and included a complete stage. The indoor pool was 80ft of tiled, graduating levels. The Winter Garden included exotic birds in cages, sprays of water and live greenery, and altogether created a tropical jungle retreat. The main lounge was decorated with glass panels by Dupas and featured the largest Aubusson carpet afloat. Each first-class cabin was done in its own unique decor, resulting in 400 different concepts and themes.

Outbound. The *Normandie* sets off from Le Havre on her maiden crossing to New York. (Author's Collection)

Two deluxe apartments, located on the Sun Deck, headed the first-class section. Each had four bedrooms, a private terrace, attached servants' quarters and a private dining salon with an individual serving area and warming kitchen. Visitors to the *Normandie* were almost always impressed with her proportions, her quality and certainly her elegance.

For image and goodwill, the *Normandie* was a huge success, a public relations dreamboat, and she did indeed convey the finest image, as a floating ambassador, for France and the French. In reality, she also had her problems and shortcomings: she suffered from vibration, lost the Blue Riband to arch-rival Britain's new *Queen Mary* in 1938 and averaged less than 60 per cent occupancy overall in her four and a half years of commercial service. The French did think of building a near-sister, a larger version at 80,000 tons that would have been called *Bretagne*, but rising war clouds over Europe in the late 1930s soon killed any such plans.

A great deal has been written, often in great detail, about the life and times of the *Normandie* (in fact my book, *Classic Liners: SS Normandie*, was published just prior to this one). Therefore, in something of a more basic review, on 28 August 1939, the French flagship was 'temporarily' laid up at New York's Pier 88. While war was officially still days away, the French were obviously not taking any risks. In a strange twist of fate and circumstance, she would never go to sea again. As the Nazi war machine advanced and with the subsequent fall of France itself in June 1940, keeping the big liner in the safety of still-neutral American waters seemed the most sensible course of action. The *Normandie* lay idle, dark and lonely, her funnels capped, her furnishings overlaid with dust covers and her 1,100 crew reduced to 115 maintenance staff.

While most of the world's liners had already begun trooping, speculation surrounded the silent *Normandie*. Would she too eventually be used as a high-capacity troopship? And for whom? Or, some suggested, would she be rebuilt as an aircraft carrier? The latter theory included sketches detailing how her innards could be stripped out, dismantled and then made into vast storage areas for aircraft. Her long hull, it was rumoured, could easily support an entire flight deck. In the end, the troopship concept was the most appropriate and least costly. She would be the third-largest Allied troop transport, carrying over 15,000 soldiers per voyage, and sail in company with the *Queen Mary* and *Queen Elizabeth*, both of which were already on war duties.

Five days after the Japanese attack on Pearl Harbor on 12 December 1941, the *Normandie* was officially seized by the US government. On 27 December, after being specifically allocated to the US Navy, she was renamed USS *Lafayette* and immediate conversion began at Pier 88, using workers from a

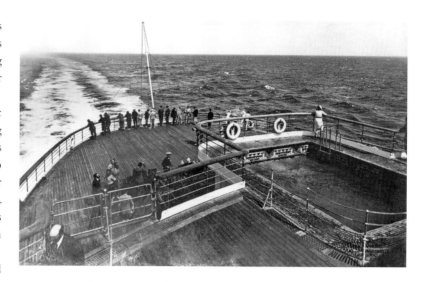

En route. Travelling at some 29 knots, the *Normandie* stern and outdoor pool are viewed during an Atlantic crossing. (Albert Wilhelmi Collection)

local shipyard. The luxurious interiors were removed, often crated and taken ashore. Some were hastily stored, however, with the assumption that the war would be over within a year. Generally, an almost incredible sense of urgency echoed over the entire project. The *Normandie/Lafayette* was scheduled to sail for Boston in mid-February, and then deliver a large contingent of servicemen to Australia via the South African Cape.

But then, just days before the projected completion of the giant ship's conversion, on the cold afternoon of 9 February 1942 fire erupted. Sparks from a workman's acetylene torch ignited a highly flammable pile of kapok life jackets. The blaze spread quickly, fanned by the winter winds blowing across the ice-filled Hudson. Workers evacuated the ship while firefighting units, both ashore and afloat, arrived at the scene. Suddenly, a blanket of brown-orange smoke hung over midtown Manhattan. Complicating matters even further, the high excitement of the *Normandie* being afire led to great misjudgement. While the fire itself created considerable damage (which most likely could have been repaired), the overzealous firefighters poured tons of water onto the fiery ship. In the early hours of the next morning, unable to withstand the added weight, the *Normandie* turned on her port side and capsized. She was lost.

Resting on her side, the giant ex-*Normandie* created the most difficult salvage job of all time. First, her funnels, masts and all of her superstructure

Festive occasion. Ten thousand balloons were released in March 1937 when five noted liners were together at New York. The *Normandie* is outbound on the left; the sterns (from top to bottom) of the *Berengaria, Georgic, Rex* and *Europa* can be seen to the right. (Cronican-Arroyo Collection)

had to be removed by floating cranes. Great pumps then pushed harbour water out of the vast, burnt-out hulk. This extraordinary operation, used as a Navy diving school exercise, and costing a staggering $5 million (£1 million), was completed in the late summer of 1943. Once righted, there were further rumours that she would finally be rebuilt as an aircraft carrier. In fact, there were no plans for the ship and, on a November morning, the powerless ship was towed downriver by a small armada of tugs. The former queen of the seas was laid up at a Brooklyn pier, quietly awaiting the end of the war. Months after the war ended, she was officially stricken from the Navy's list of ships in October 1945. She passed into the hands of the US Maritime Commission,

which had no interest in the ship. Her original Russian designer, Vladimir Yourkevitch, put forth his plan to cut the ship in two, reduce its size and rebuild her with two funnels. No one, not even the French, were interested.

In October 1946, she was sold to a local New York Harbor scrap metal firm (for a mere $161,000 (£40,000)) and a month later was towed, almost grotesquely, across the Lower Bay to Port Newark, New Jersey, for dismantling. Within twelve months, the last remains of that ship of genius, style and distinction were gone. She was twelve years old but had actually sailed for only four and a half years. The site where she was finished off is still a busy scrap metal depot.

8

SOLDIERS ALONG THE DECKS: THE *PASTEUR*

An ocean liner enthusiast friend always referred to the *Pasteur* as 'the ship with the big stack'. Indeed, she had one of the very tallest funnels ever to go to sea. Another friend saw her at Marseilles in 1957. He was arriving from Melbourne and heading for London on P&O's *Arcadia*. He spotted a liner moored and obviously laid up in the outer harbour. Scratching his head, he soon recognised the liner because of that towering funnel. It was the *Pasteur*.

The Compagnie de Navigation Sud-Atlantique hoped to make their brand-new *Pasteur* the most luxurious as well as the fastest liner in Europe–South America service. She would outpace the likes of Germany's *Cap Arcona*, Italy's *Augustus* and *Roma*, and even Britain's brand-new *Andes*. Descriptive literature all but flooded the interested market in the spring and summer of 1939, heralding the new 'queen' of the South Atlantic, the long-awaited replacement for the 42,000-ton *L'Atlantique*, tragically destroyed by fire when less than two years old in January 1933. If the *Pasteur* was somewhat smaller, at 30,000 tons, she was equally as interesting and well decorated. Her maiden trip was set for early September 1939, from Bordeaux to Rio, Santos, Montevideo and Buenos Aires. Then, quite suddenly, events farther east in Poland changed everything. As war dramatically and unexpectedly erupted, the maiden voyage was cancelled and the liner sent to Brest for temporary safety. In preparation for wartime use, all of her brand-new, luxurious fittings and furnishings were removed, sent to storage at St Nazaire and then sold off long after the war, in 1951.

On orders from the French government, the 697ft-long *Pasteur* finally returned to the sea eight months later, in May 1940. It was just weeks before the Nazi invasion of France. The *Pasteur* was ordered to Halifax with a special cargo: over 200 tons of gold, carefully disguised in burlap bags, from the French National Reserves. In all, using several warships as well, some 2,300 tons of gold was hurriedly moved to Canada for safekeeping. Afterwards, the *Pasteur* was sent down to New York, joining the idle *Normandie* at the French Line's Pier 88, to await further orders. Soon, and after the fall of France was fully realised, she was passed over to British operation and placed in the expert management hands of Cunard-White Star. Her subsequent role was largely trooping, often on the North Atlantic and in company with the *Île de France*. At times, the *Pasteur* – built originally for a capacity of 751 peacetime passengers – sailed with over 5,000 on board.

By the war's end in the summer of 1945, the *Pasteur* had a distinctive record – she had carried over 300,000 troops in five years of war service. She was officially returned by the British to the French a year later, in April 1946. Thereafter owned by the French government, and only managed by her former owners, she was still painted in Sud-Atlantique colours. There was brief thought given to restoring her for liner service, but she was immediately detoured to French Indo–China for further trooping and return evacuation service. As political problems there increased, any thought of a return to commercial status became more remote. Alone, between 1947 and 1953,

Worn and tired. The *Pasteur* seen just after the war ended in late 1945. (Albert Wilhelmi Collection)

Carrying troops, the *Pasteur* – with her towering funnel so evident – passes through the Suez Canal on a return voyage from Saigon to Marseilles. (Cronican-Arroyo Collection)

she made thirty-nine round trips between Marseilles or Toulon and Tonkin (because of her deep draft she was unable to go upriver directly to Saigon). The 'world's largest peacetime troopship' was not decommissioned from troop duties until January 1957, twelve years after the war ended. She was even chartered to the Dutch in 1950, bringing home troops from troubled Indonesia. In 1956, the *Pasteur* was placed on shorter runs by the French, carrying troops from Algeria and the Suez.

Laid up and awaiting future plans, the *Pasteur* was looked over by the French Line for possible conversion to a liner, more specifically to replace the ageing *Île de France* on the Le Havre–New York run. Such a transformation would be costly, at an estimated 6 million francs, and so instead a decision was made to build a brand-new, even more costly, large liner, which became the *France* and launched in 1960. In the end, there was no place for the *Pasteur* under the Tricolour. In the summer of 1957, the French government announced that seven French passenger ships would be sold to foreign buyers to bring in badly needed foreign currency. Among them was the 17,300grt *La Marseillaise*, the former flagship of Messageries Maritimes, and the idle *Pasteur*.

After 99 per cent of its fleet had either been destroyed or confiscated as reparations, North German Lloyd was more than reawakened by the mid-fifties. Their first post-war liner, the 19,000grt *Berlin*, the former *Gripsholm* of 1925, had reopened West German service to New York and was immensely popular. NGL was anxious to expand. They saw great potential in the *Pasteur*, bought her in September 1957 and had her moved to Bremen for thorough rebuilding and refitting as a luxury liner. The 23-knot ship was all but completely gutted and reduced to a bare hulk. New turbines went aboard which could produce a very reputable 23 knots (or, as NGL publicists noted, the equivalent of 2,000 Volkswagens operating together); there was improved wiring throughout, plumbing installed and accomodations fitted that were as complete as in any other Atlantic liner of the day. Buoyant times continued on that trans-ocean run – the Dutch were adding their 38,000grt *Rotterdam*, Italy was building the 33,000grt *Leonardo da Vinci*, Cunard was making plans for a 75,000-ton replacement for the ageing *Queen Mary* and, of course, the French were constructing the 66,000-ton *France*.

Rechristened *Bremen*, long considered as Germany's most distinguished sea name, the 1,122-berth liner set course for New York from Bremerhaven and via Southampton and Cherbourg in July 1959. Her position as a superb vessel, highlighted by impeccable German service and maintenance, was quickly established. It was quite coincidental that on her maiden arrival, the former French *Bremen* was docked just across Pier 88's shed from the former German *Liberté*. In the winter months, the *Bremen* – with a reduced, all-first-class capacity and a portable outdoor pool affixed to an aft deck – travelled south to the sun, on mostly two-week itineraries around the Caribbean.

North German Lloyd merged, in 1971, with the Hamburg America Line and created Hapag-Lloyd, one of the world's mightiest shipping firms. It was a union of economies in the ever-increasing competitiveness of the international maritime industry. An early decision was to discontinue the diminished, money-losing transatlantic liner run, concentrate instead on cruising and retire the ageing, mechanically troublesome *Bremen*. Her engine failures caused delays and even cancelled sailings, which did little to maintain the company's otherwise impeccable image.

The ex-*Pasteur* would have a third career – she was sold to Greek-owned Chandris Cruises at the end of 1971 and became their *Regina Magna* ('the Big Queen'), which was not be confused with the smaller *Regina* (ex-*Panama*, ex-*President Hoover*), which was soon renamed *Regina Prima* to end any confusion.

Carrying up to 900 one-class passengers, the *Regina Magna* was sent cruising year-round, beginning in the summer of 1972, from Amsterdam and London to Scandinavia and from Genoa to West Africa and around the Mediterranean. Still later, there were winter trips in the Caribbean, departing from Curacao and San Juan. However, even for the very methodical, cost-conscious Chandris Company, the ship's machinery was proving costly as well as troublesome and then international fuel oil costs suddenly soared from $35 (£24) to $95 (£70) a ton. After a mere two summers, by autumn 1974, the *Regina Magna* was laid up at Perama, near Piraeus, with a good assortment of other passenger ships, all mostly unwanted, past their best and nearing their end. The *Regina Magna* sat quietly, nested between some out-of-work tankers. She had little hope of further sailing.

She managed, however, through some form of good fortune, to find a buyer (the Philippine-Singapore Ports Corporation) in 1977. On 6 October, she departed from Piraeus for Jeddah, Saudi Arabia, for use as a permanently moored accommodation centre. Under the flag of the Philippines as the renamed *Saudi Phil I*, she was used as part of a major construction project, housing up to 3,600 workers at one time. She actually changed names one more time, in March 1978, to *Filipinas Saudi I*.

When this Arabian work project ended in 1980, her only alternative – at the age of forty-one and with those faulty engines and by then greatly deteriorated condition – was the scrapyards. She was sold, placed under tow and routed out to Kaohsiung on Taiwan. Early in this voyage, on 6 June, however, the slow-moving, former French-German-Greek-Philippine liner suddenly heeled over and sank at sea, making for a quick end to her long and varied life.

9

POST-WAR SPLENDOURS:
THE *ÎLE DE FRANCE* AND *LIBERTÉ*

The late Lewis Gordon and his wife made over 100 crossings of the Atlantic, a pattern that began with their honeymoon in 1937. He knew, I always felt, the Atlantic liners very intimately and had a keen eye for observation. He liked many ships, for example the *Caronia* and the Italian liners of the '50s, but he just loved the French Line:

> In first class in the 1950s on board the *Île de France* and *Liberté*, you had the finest decor, the most spectacular food and the best dressed passengers on all the seas. The French Line was style, glamour, absolutely chic. And those two ships had great ambience – they offered the gayest crossings on the Atlantic. The 6-day voyages even seemed to go faster than on any other ships. The *France*, which appeared in 1962 and replaced the earlier team, was quite wonderful, but not quite the same. The *Île de France* and, perhaps even slightly more so, the *Liberté* were two of our all-time favourite Atlantic liners!

The *Île de France* was a heroic, heavily used ship during the Second World War; the *Europa/Liberté* sat out the entire period in idleness. The *Île* was abruptly pulled out of Atlantic liner service and laid up in the autumn of 1939. The French, like most of Europe, were worried about Nazi plans. The prized *Île* could not return home, at least on orders from a tense French government. She was shifted from Pier 88 to a berth on Staten Island, waiting under the watchful eye of a much-reduced crew of 100. Then, on 1 May 1940, after being loaned to the British Ministry of Transport, she sailed to Europe with precious war materials, including several uncrated bombers, and then on to Singapore. Once

France fell to the enemy in the spring of 1940, the *Île* was officially seized – sailing thereafter under the dual flags of Free France and Britain.

Out in the East, the 791ft-long liner was ported at Saigon and later at Bombay. She sailed with a mostly Asiatic crew and was under the wartime management of the famed P&O Lines. Trooping in grey colouring, she worked in tandem with two similar-sized liners, Cunard's *Mauretania* and the Dutch *Nieuw Amsterdam*, sailing mostly on the Cape Town-to-Suez

Bound for Southampton and Le Havre. The majestic *Île de France* sails from New York in this view from the early 1950s. (Moran Towing & Transportation Company)

troop and evacuation shuttle. Then, in 1943, she was shifted back onto the North Atlantic, changed to Cunard management and sailed in company with another French liner, the *Pasteur*.

The *Île* was heroically decommissioned in September 1945 from official wartime duties. She turned to 'austerity service' between Cherbourg, New York and sometimes Halifax, and then did some trooping out to politically troubled French Indo-China. It was not until the spring of 1947 that she was back at the St Nazaire shipyard for a massive rebuilding and restoration to a luxury passenger ship. She inherited much of the old glamour and some of the *Normandie*'s flawless furnishings, and even had her three original stacks replaced by two of modern proportions. Her quarters were reconfigured for 1,345 passengers (541 first class, 577 cabin class and 227 tourist class). She steamed into New York Harbor in the summer of 1949 to a gala reception and on something of a 'second maiden voyage'.

With a revised, increased tonnage, the 44,356grt *Île* quickly settled down to further service (and hefty post-war profits) along with the larger *Liberté* and the smaller, more tourist-oriented *Flandre*. The *Île* remained unique (even among all Atlantic liners of the '50s), terribly popular and made still more headlines. On 26 July 1956, off Nantucket, she rescued 753 survivors from the sinking *Andrea Doria*, which was fatally wounded after a collision with Sweden's *Stockholm*. In October of that same year, she was lashed by a ferocious Atlantic storm, one that flooded six passenger cabins and dented the superstructure. Still later, in February 1957, she went aground on Martinique during a winter Caribbean cruise. Her passengers had to be flown home and the liner towed all the way to a shipyard at Newport News, Virginia, for lengthy repairs.

The *Île* – with her passenger lists finally beginning to dwindle – reached her well-deserved retirement in November 1958. The French Line offices in Paris were faced with a variety of prospects for their famed ship. Some wanted her as a museum, the Sheraton Company talked of using her as a floating hotel in the Caribbean, and one imaginative enthusiast suggested cutting her down and then sailing her straight into the heart of Paris. In the end, she was sold to Japanese shipbreakers, who sailed her out, under the Japanese flag, to Osaka as the *Furansu Maru* (France Maru).

Summer sailing. After a late morning departure from Pier 88, the *Île de France* passes Lower Manhattan. (Port Authority of New York & New Jersey)

Grand style. The handsome Cafe de Paris aboard the *Île de France*. (Author's Collection)

The ship's first-class library – a perfect place to read a book! (Author's Collection)

The bedroom of the *Ile*'s Fontainebleau Suite. (Author's Collection)

Passing the Statue of Liberty, the *Île de France* is outward bound in New York Harbor's Upper Bay; the *Berlin* is just behind, on the far left. (French Line)

The end for the beloved *Île de France* was not as gentle as the French Line would have liked, however. The Japanese chartered the liner, at the rate of $4,000 (£1,000) per day, to a Hollywood film company. Robert Stack, Dorothy Malone and hundreds of others climbed aboard to make *The Last Voyage*, a fictional tale of an aged trans-Pacific liner that melodramatically explodes on its final run. Studio technicians blasted away at the lounges, gutted some of the former suites and even released the forward funnel and sent it crashing down into the wheelhouse. The French Line was furious: was there no respect for an Atlantic legend, a French goddess of the seas? It succeeded, following quick court action, to at least have the ship's red-and-black funnels painted over. Finally, with the filming complete, she went back to Osaka for the final dismantling.

Bigger than the *Île de France*, the 51,839grt *Liberté* came to the French as post-war reparations, largely as compensation of a sort for the loss of the *Normandie*. In May 1945, just as Nazi Germany collapsed in defeat, invading American forces entered the seaport of Bremerhaven and all but raced to the docks. Their prize was the third largest liner afloat, the *Europa* of pre-war North German Lloyd fame and distinction. She had been one of the most fabled ocean queens of the 1930s and reigned, if briefly,

A joyous occasion. The newly refitted *Liberté*, now flagship of the French Line, arrives in New York for the first time in August 1950. Italy's *Conte Biancamano* is docked in the background, at Pier 84. (Cronican-Arroyo Collection)

Departing on her eastbound maiden crossing, on 25 August 1950, the *Liberté* passes the inbound *Île de France*. The two great ships are just off West 35th Street, in mid-Hudson River. (Cronican-Arroyo Collection)

High splendour. The first-class grand salon on board the 51,000grt *Liberté*. (Author's Collection)

The Music Room in first class, on board the *Liberté*. (Author's Collection)

Luxury on the high seas. The sitting room of the Normandie Apartment de Luxe aboard the 936ft-long *Liberté*. (Author's Collection)

as the world's fastest ship. By the war's end, the likes of the super-class *Rex*, *Conte di Savoia*, *Empress of Britain*, *Normandie* and the *Bremen*, the *Europa*'s near-sister, were all gone, senselessly destroyed. By 1945, only Britain's *Queen Mary* and *Queen Elizabeth* were larger than the *Europa*.

The US soldiers that boarded the 936ft-long liner saw little to reflect the glamour and opulence of bygone times. Instead, they found a rusting, neglected, ill-kept vessel held from sea for almost six years (since September 1939) and one seemingly passed by during the war years. Yellowing signs were still posted throughout, meant to direct the Nazi soldiers that never quite came aboard. At other times, Berlin had planned to make her over as an aircraft carrier or use her as a giant landing ship for the planned invasion of Britain which never happened. As the war regressed for Hitler, any role for the 24-knot, quadruple-screw *Europa* became more remote. Towards the very end, in April 1945, an order from the Nazi high command was given to destroy the liner, but following a change of mind, or stroke of disobedience, it was never carried out.

Luxury Liner Row. A busy day on 9 July 1958, with eight liners in port together (from left to right): *Britannic*, *Queen Elizabeth*, *Mauretania*, *Liberté*, *United States*, *America*, *Independence* and *Vulcania*. (Port Authority of New York & New Jersey)

Together at Le Havre, the *Île de France* is on the left and the *Liberté* on the right. (Richard Faber Collection)

French Line, like Messageries Maritimes and other French shipping lines, operated a good number of freighters that carried up to twelve passengers. Seen off Dover, this is the 1949-built *Cavalier de la Salle*. (Author's Collection)

The 20,000grt *Flandre* was French Line's first new-build for their Le Havre–New York service, following the losses of the Second World War. (Albert Wilhelmi Collection)

While far smaller than the *Île de France* and *Liberté*, the *Flandre* was very popular and had a following of her own. Seen here at Le Havre, the *America* is berthed to the right. (Author's Collection)

Nested together during a seamen's strike, the *Flandre* (left) and *Antilles* (right) were almost identical sister ships. (Albert Wilhelmi Collection)

Left: Burnt out and badly damaged, the remains of the Greek cruise ship *Pallas Athena*, the former *Flandre*, are seen outside Piraeus harbour in Greece. The date is July 1994. (Frank Heine Collection)

Below: The smart-looking *Antilles* later had her funnel heightened, which gave her a more definitive appearance compared to her otherwise twin sister *Flandre*. (Author's Collection)

The Americans quickly dubbed the ship as *AP-177*, the USS *Europa*. After a quick cleaning and some brief tryouts, she was ready for sea duty. She left Bremerhaven for New York on her first troop crossing in September 1945, with 4,300 soldiers and 960 crew on board. Sensibly, she was given a forty-five-day overhaul at a Bayonne, New Jersey shipyard after reaching New York. It seemed she would be very useful – it was calculated she could be run at as much as 28 knots while repatriating as many as 20,000 troops per month.

But there was trouble ahead. The USS *Europa* had hardly completed a few voyages when she was plagued by a serious problem: fires. They seemed to be endless and at least one lasted a full nine hours. On another day, no less than five outbreaks had to be fought and extinguished. An investigative team discovered that the Nazis had removed much of her original, 1930-installed materials, especially as shortages developed in the waning days of battle. The replacements were inferior. Furthermore, serious hull cracking was uncovered, much of it dating back to the '30s under North German Lloyd operation. Quickly deemed unwanted by the Americans, she was handed over to the United Nations Reparations Commission, who soon passed the ship to the French.

She hoisted the Tricolour, was thoughtfully renamed *Liberté* (although *Lorraine*, *Liberation* and even *La Liberté* were among earlier, if brief, considerations) and was moved to Le Havre to await refitting for French Line luxury service. But then she ran into more trouble. During a ferocious gale in December 1946, she was ripped from her Le Havre moorings and thrown against the sunken hull of the liner *Paris* (left untouched since April 1939). A huge gash in the *Liberté*'s hull caused her to flood, cant over, then be righted and finally settle in an upright position. All restoration was temporarily shunted aside; salvage became the priority. Eventually the hole was plugged and the ship moved to the giant shipyard at St Nazaire. Refitting would take over three years.

To become a French liner in the glamorous, stylised tradition of the likes of the *Normandie* and *Île de France* meant heavy cosmetic surgery for the *Liberté*. Most of all, she had to be 'de-Germanised'. The work was costly, slow and often delayed. She finally emerged in the summer of 1950 as a grand and glorious example of late Art Deco, sumptuously fitted with an array of first-class suites and superb restaurants. One regular passenger told me, 'The *Liberté* had many virtues including the finest wine cellar at sea back in the 1950s.' She could cross between New York and Le Havre, with a quick stop at Plymouth or Southampton, in six days. Fares in 1950 were $345 (£115) in first class, $220 (£70) in cabin class and $165 (£55) in tourist. Along her decks strolled the likes of Greta Garbo and Elizabeth Taylor, European duchesses and Arabian princes, and of course any number of 'commuting' tycoons and heiresses. Even after the introduction of speedy jet travel in October 1958, the *Liberté* managed to retain her popularity.

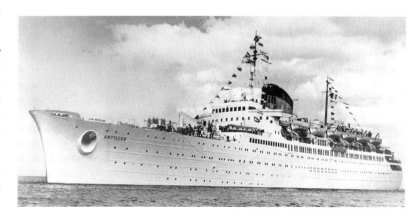

The original, flattish funnels were enhanced in 1954 with new domed tops. This made the stacks taller and added to the ship's towering appearance, a sense of seagoing might and majesty. It was almost a top-heavy look, and most likely induced romantic images of just how enormous great liners actually were.

In the late 1950s, as the *Liberté* went to St Nazaire for her annual check-up, she would be in sight of her eventual replacement, the 66,000grt *France*, then under construction. Finally, in November 1961, the older ship sailed from New York for the last time. She had a grand send-off: tugs, fireboats and bellowing whistles from other ships in the port. At nearly thirty-two, she left a great memory. The end came the following spring at the hands of shipbreakers at La Spezia in Italy.

During the 1950s, the third French liner, the sidekick of sorts to the *Île de France* and *Liberté*, was a smaller ship, the 20,400grt *Flandre*. When I sailed aboard Costa Cruises' *Carla Costa* back in April 1983, I especially looked over the 600-footer for traces, even hints, of her past. In fact, there was very little. I remembered her from earlier days, when she regularly sailed in and out of New York as the 'smart-looking' *Flandre*. By the time I sailed in her, she was an all-white, contemporary cruise ship – still quite sleek, with modern interiors, a happy crew and rather good Italian kitchens.

Built at Dunkirk in 1952, the 784-passenger ship was then part of France's post-Second World War rebuilding program me. Initially planned for the colonial West Indies trade, she was soon separated from her sister, the *Antilles*

(which burned and sank in the Caribbean in January 1971), and instead the 20-knot *Flandre* was used on a far less tropical route, sailing the North Atlantic between Le Havre, Southampton and New York. She carried her passengers in three classes – 402 in first class, 285 in cabin and a rather meagre 97 in tourist. A peak season first-class fare in 1961 for a seven-day crossing was priced from $360 (£120). In the winter, when the Atlantic could grow fierce, even ferocious, and passengers were scarce, the *Flandre* was detoured to that intended Caribbean service.

In her early years, the *Flandre* was teamed with the far larger, fancier, highly reputed pair of *Île de France* and *Liberté*. Seemingly misplaced, the smaller ship held her own and was actually quite popular. Later, but then only for a year (1962), she was paired with the brand-new *France*. But as the Atlantic passenger trade steadily declined, the *Flandre* turned to West Indies sailings full time before being put up for sale in 1968.

Costa bought her, had her completely restyled as a cruise ship and then rechristened her *Carla 'C'*. She was, in fact, chartered in 1969–70 to the newly formed, Los Angeles-based Princess Cruises who advertised her as the *Princess Carla*, even though she hadn't been formally renamed. Cruise hostess Jeraldine Saunders penned her first chapters of *Love Boat* on board the *Princess Carla*.

Later renamed *Carla Costa*, she was sold to Greek-owned Epirotiki Lines in 1992 and rechristened *Pallas Athena*. She burned out at Piraeus in March 1994, was uneconomic to repair and then broken up a year later in Turkey.

Busy day at Le Havre in July 1957. On the right, the *Colombie* is departing; the *Liberté* is behind; and the *Arosa Sun* and *Arosa Sky* are to the left. (Philippe Brebant Collection)

Passenger liners at Le Havre in 1950. Holland America's *Nieuw Amsterdam* is on the left and the *Europa* of the Incres Line is to the right. (Philippe Brebant Collection)

Above: A poster from the 1920s for French Line's Europe–Gulf of Mexico service. (Author's Collection)

Above right: A superb painting by artist J. Gille, of the *Île de France* returning to St Nazaire in 1947 for her conversion for luxury service following heroic war duties. (Author's Collection)

Right: The *Île de France* departing from New York. (Author's Collection)

Above: A poster issued for the maiden arrival of the *Liberté* in 1950. (Author's Collection)

Left: A 1950s poster for French Line's service to New York. (Author's Collection)

A Moran tug guides the *Liberté* from New York's Pier 88.
(Author's Collection)

A pre-war postcard view of Paquet's *Djenne*. (Albert Wilhelmi
Collection)

Left: Eastern waters: The *Felix Roussel* arriving in Saigon. (Author's Collection)

Opposite: 1930s style – a poster of Paquet's steamer *Marechal Lyuatey.* (Author's Collection)

Below: Another fine painting from artist J. Gille, this one of the troopship *Pasteur* in Indo-Chinese waters. (Author's Collection)

Cie DE NAVIGATION PAQUET

"MARÉCHAL LYAUTEY"

MAROC
SÉNÉGAL
LEVANT &
MER NOIRE
PAR MARSEILLE

M PONTY

The combo liner *Louis Lumière*, used in Chargeurs Reunis service to South America. (Author's Collection)

The *Cambodge* of Messageries Maritimes was later converted to the Greek-flag cruise ship *Stella Solaris*. (Author's Collection)

Another former Messageries Maritimes combo liner, the *Tahitien*, was rebuilt in the early 1970s as the Greek cruise ship *Atalante*. (Med Sun Lines)

AROSA LINE

»AROSA SKY«

DIENST

SCHNELL

EUROPA

NORDAMERIKA

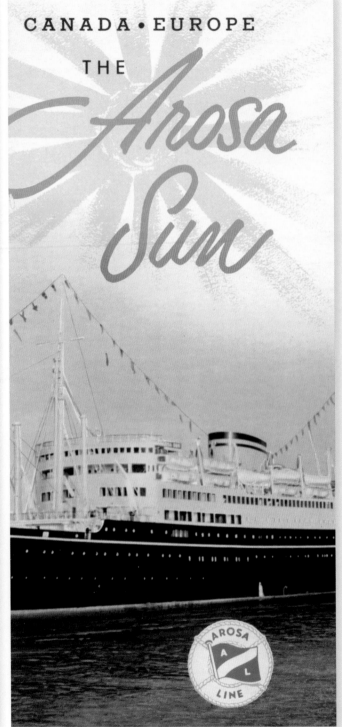

CANADA · EUROPE

THE

Arosa Sun

AROSA LINE

Above: A fine painting of Paquet's *Djenne*. (Albert Wilhelmi Collection)

Opposite left: A brochure cover featuring the *Arosa Sky*, the former French *La Marseillaise*. (Author's Collection)

Opposite right: Another Arosa Line brochure from the late 1950s, this one highlighting the *Arosa Sun*, the one-time *Felix Roussel*. (Author's Collection)

Another splendid painting: this one of the *Koutoubia,* also of Paquet. (Albert Wilhelmi Collection)

The *Azrou* of Paquet sailed in West African service. (Albert Wilhelmi Collection)

Right: A handsome view of the *Azemmour,* also of Paquet. (Albert Wilhelmi Collection)

Below: The innovative *El Djezair* with her engines-aft design. (Albert Wilhelmi Collection)

Above: An evocative view of the *El Mansour* of Compagnie de Navigaion Mixte. (Albert Wilhelmi Collection)

The *Provence* of Transports Maritimes was created for service to Latin America from Marseilles. (Albert Wilhelmi Collection)

The 1950-built *Provence* later became the *Symphony* for Italy's MSC Cruises. Shown here in 1999 at Malta, her fleetmate *Rhapsody*, the former *Cunard Princess*, is on the left. (Michael Cassar)

The brand-new *Jean Mermoz* leaving St Nazaire in 1957. (Albert Wilhelmi Collection)

The *Jean Mermoz* was rebuilt in 1970 as the cruise ship *Mermoz*. (Bodhan Huras)

Another view of the long popular *Mermoz*. (Jurgen Saupe)

In this aerial view of Piraeus Harbour in Greece, the *City of Athens*, the former French Line *Ville de Tunis*, is docked in the centre position. (Author's Collection)

A brochure for the *City of Athens'* Aegean service. (Author's Collection)

The striking *Renaissance*, but in her later years as Epirotiki Lines' *World Renaissance*. (Luis Miguel Correia)

Above: The *France* at Le Havre. (Albert Wilhelmi Collection)

Opposite: A fine aerial view of the 66,348grt *France* at Le Havre. (Albert Wilhelmi Collection)

THE NEW
S.S. FRANCE

IN SERVICE EARLY 1962

French Line

COMPAGNIE GENERALE TRANSATLANTIQUE

A brochure heralding the maiden arrival of the *France* in 1962. (Author's Collection)

Above: The *France* at Le Havre on a summer afternoon. (Albert Wilhelmi Collection)

Right: The magnificent first-class Chambord restaurant on board the *France.* (Albert Wilhelmi Collection)

The ship's 664-seat movie theatre. (Albert Wilhelmi Collection)

The first-class smoking room. (Albert Wilhelmi Collection)

The first-class bar. (Albert Wilhelmi Collection)

The tourist-class main lounge. (Albert Wilhelmi Collection)

The children's playroom. (Albert Wilhelmi Collection)

The first-class Promenade Deck. (Albert Wilhelmi Collection)

The bedroom of the lavish Normandie Suite. (Albert Wilhelmi Collection)

The tourist-class children's dining room. (Albert Wilhelmi Collection)

The luxurious indoor swimming pool. (Albert Wilhelmi Collection)

Artist Don Stoltenberg's evocative night-time rendition of the stylised *France*. (Don Stoltenberg Collection)

A fine painting of the maiden arrival in New York of the *France*. (Author's Collection)

Bon voyage! The *France* departs from New York. (Photograph by Fred Rodriguez)

New York-based ocean liner memorabilia collector and dealer Richard Faber displays a CGT/French Line houseflag as the *Norway* (ex-*France*) departs from New York in September 2001. (Richard Faber Collection)

Another of artist Don Stoltenberg's superb depictions of the great *France*. (Don Stoltenberg Collection)

10

MESSAGERIES MARITIMES AND 'THE THREE MUSKETEERS'

French passenger ships offered worldwide services up until the 1960s. One could travel just about anywhere on a French-flag ship. The late Marion Seeth was married to a New York Harbor pilot, but was adventurous in her own right – she would set off on long, interconnecting sea voyages, often going right round the world. One spring in the 1960s, she travelled from New York to Cannes aboard the *Constitution*. From there, she connected at Marseilles to the *Cambodge* for the long voyage out to Yokohama in Japan. It was notable becasue not many New Yorkers travelled on ships such as the *Cambodge* and, as an American, she would have been a definite minority on board that Messageries Maritimes combo liner. From Yokohama she crossed to San Francisco on the *President Wilson* before taking a train home to New York. What an adventure – I recall her telling me it took four months in all!

While Messageries Maritimes were noted, especially in the 1920s and '30s, for their rather eccentric exterior design and highly stylised, Asian-themed interiors, the company chose a more contemporary style after the Second World War. Their primary interest lay with practical passenger-cargo liners –

Flagship to the Far East. The rather short-lived 17,000grt *La Marseillaise* of Messageries Maritimes. Completed in 1949, she was sold off in 1957. (Albert Wilhelmi Collection)

three for the Marseilles–Far East run, two for the South Pacific and Australia, and a quartet to Mauritius and Indian Ocean ports. The trio for the Far East were perhaps the finest and certainly the best looking. Named for three 'Free States' of the so-called French Union, the handsome ships came into service in 1952–54 as the *Viet-Nam*, *Cambodge* and *Laos*. They were dubbed the 'Three Musketeers'.

Built in French shipyards, based on government loans, at Dunkirk and at La Ciotat, they were good-sized ships for their day – 13,200 tons and 532ft in length. Passenger-cargo liners were very popular in the decade or so after the Second World War and these new French sisters matched, say, Cunard's *Media* and *Parthia* and the Ellerman Lines' *City of Port Elizabeth* quartet. Painted completely in white and capped by all-white, domed, single stacks, their extended superstructures were in the centre. Masts, booms and hatches were both fore and aft. The trio carried general cargo outwards; mainly lots of French-manufactured goods, including Citroën automobiles, as well as large consignments of mail. Homewards, their manifests included timber, tinned fish, rubber, latex, palm oil, silk and the beginning waves of the mass-produced items coming out of the East.

Elegance and comfort in Eastern waters. The first-class veranda cafe on board the *La Marseillaise*. (Author's Collection)

The former French *Felix Roussel* later sailed as the Atlantic liner *Arosa Sun* for the short-lived Arosa Line. She is seen here at Hamburg. (Arnold Kludas Collection)

The *La Marseillaise* also joined the Swiss-owned Arosa Line and sailed as their flagship *Arosa Sky*. (Author's Collection)

Great examples of 1950s passenger-cargo liner design, the *Cambodge* and her two sisters were fine and popular additions to the Europe–Far East service. (Albert Wilhelmi Collection)

Fast ships powered by steam turbines, they often exceeded their 21-knot service speeds to maintain their monthly sailing schedule from Marseilles. They were routed to Port Said, the Suez Canal, Aden, Djibouti, Bombay, Colombo, Singapore, Saigon, Manila, Hong Kong, Kobe and then turned around at Yokohama to do the same route in reverse.

In their passenger quarters, the owners opted for modern French decor. The first-class main lounge was, for example, done in soft colours and highlighted by vividly painted Chinese dragons. The floors were inlaid with fine woods and this space adjoined a small music room. Folding doors in the bar could be opened, giving it a true tropical flavour, certainly one reminiscent of French colonial Saigon. There was also a small writing room, a veranda and a blue-tiled outdoor pool that could be floodlit for night-time use. The dining room was notable, especially for its descending stairwell, a design feature so often used by the French – and used so well. As in second class, the first-class restaurant doubled as an evening cinema. All of the first-class staterooms had private bathrooms (at least a shower and toilet, but many with tub baths as well) and were praised in some travel journals for their detailed, thoughtful outfitting. This included a luggage rack, a folding chair (which, when not in use, fitted into a flush position), several reading lamps (at various angles and elevations), wide beds and, unusually for the '50s, no call buttons but instead actual telephones. The cabins *de luxe* included full bathrooms as well as sitting areas. All first-class cabins, as well as the first-class dining room, were air-conditioned (as were the inside tourist class staterooms).

Berthing was arranged for 117 first class, 110 tourist class and 314 third class. In the early 1960s, the full round-trip fare for seventy-five days was $1,500 (£550).

In the 1960s, as Messageries Mritimes' passenger trade began to wane, their Europe–Middle and Far Eastern voyages were often included as segments of long tours, 'around the world by ship', and these sometimes used three or four different ships including the *Queen Mary*, *Queen Elizabeth* and even the *France*. Club Med began taking great numbers of cabins and booking these Eastern voyages as long, informal, getaway holidays. This Eastern service was further complicated in the late '60s when, with the Suez Canal temporarily closed, the ships had to be rerouted around the South African Cape, calling at Cape Town and Durban. Coupled with increased airline competition (jumbo jets began to regularly go east of Suez by the late '60s), their cargos switched to some of the first generation containerships. The days of the 'Three Musketeers' were numbered.

Politically sensitive, the *Viet-Nam* became the *Pacifique* in 1968. By 1970, time had run out and all three ships were withdrawn. They left French registry and were sold off. The *Cambodge* seems to have been the most fortunate, being sold to the Greek-owned Sun Line and then being thoroughly rebuilt as the cruise ship *Stella Solaris*. She resumed sailing in June 1973 with all-new accommodation and public rooms, a large Lido Deck and 765 first-class berths replacing much of the original cargo spaces. By 1995,

Far-off waters. The *Tahitien* and her sister *Caledonien* were also fine combo liners, but served the Caribbean, the South Pacific and Australia. (Author's Collection)

Combo style. Belonging to Chargeurs Reunis and used on the Marseilles–Southeast Asia run were three 540-passenger ships: the *Edouard Branley* (shown here), *Henri Poincare* and *Clement Ader*. They dated from the early 1950s and weighed in at just over 11,000 tons. (Captain J.F. Puyvelde)

Also belonging to Chargeurs Reunis were the sisters *Lavoisier* (seen outbound at Le Havre) and *Claude Bernard*. They were used on the North Europe–East Coast of South America run and carried ninety-four passengers in first class and 230 in third class. (Albert Wilhelmi Collection)

she was dividing her time between summers in the Aegean and Eastern Mediterranean, and the remainder in Caribbean–South American waters. In two careers, she endured for fifty years before being scrapped in 2003.

The *Pacifique* and *Laos* had a very different fate. They were sold as a pair in 1970 to little-known Compania Navigacion Abeto SA, a firm that was based in the Far East, used the Panamanian flag and had interests in Far Eastern passenger service as well as the Moslem religious pilgrim trade. The *Pacifique* was renamed *Princess Abeto* and was rebuilt at Hong Kong with space for 1,612 passengers, most of which were in austere pilgrim sections. She was soon leased to a relatively unknown Eastern ship operator, the Fir Line. She was renamed *Malaysia Baru* and then *Malaysia Kita* for sailings between Singapore and Jeddah in Saudi Arabia, and later for sailings to India. Like many French and French-built ships before her, she caught fire on 12 May 1974 while undergoing repairs at Singapore. She was towed to the outer harbour, allowed to sink and burn out, and then left for almost a year. Fully refloated in the summer of 1975, her fire-ravaged remains then sat around for another year before being towed to Kaohsiung, Taiwan, and scrapped.

The *Laos* was rebuilt by Abeto as the renamed *Empress Abeto* and with a similarly large capacity for up to 1,696. She too was later chartered to the Fir Line and sailed for them as the *Malaysia Raya*. She was lying at Port Kelang on 24 August 1976 when fire broke out. Damaged beyond repair, she was towed to Kaohsiung for breaking up in the summer of 1977, one year after her former sister.

Other Messageries Maritimes passenger ships were the 12,700grt sisters *Caledonien* and *Tahitien*, which were used on the Marseilles–Caribbean–Panama–South Pacific–Australia route, and a quartet of 10,900-ton sisters used on the Marseilles–East Africa–Indian Ocean run: *Ferdinand des Lesseps*, *Jean La Borde*, *La Bourdonnais* and *Pierre Loti*.

Left: Heading for Rio. For the Marseilles–South America run, there were the 1950-built sisters *Provence* (seen here departing Naples) and her sister *Bretagne*. At 16,000 tons each, they belonged to Transports Maritimes. (Richard Faber Collection)

Below: The Nouvelle Compagnie Havraise Peninsulaire de Navigation had three combo ships sailing from mostly Northern European ports to East Africa and Indian Ocean islands. Built between 1949 and 1951, the *Île de la Reunion* (seen here), *Île Maurice* and *Nossi-Be* carried twenty-seven first-class passengers each. (Author's Collection).

11

EXPRESS TO NORTH AFRICA AND BEYOND

My Spanish teacher at high school married a young lady from Belgium and they visited her family together every summer. They often crossed on the Holland America Line, conveniently landing at either Le Havre or Rotterdam, and then drove to a small town near Brussels. He would tantalisingly tell me of his summer plans, especially about the ships. One summer, they booked a nine-night crossing on the Holland America combo liner *Prinses Margriet* and then hurried home in time for the early September reopening of school on a very fast, five-day passage aboard the *United States*. They rarely, if ever, flew and even booked a round trip through Marseilles on the French passenger ship *Kairouan* to visit relatives in North Africa. I went over to the French Line offices at Rockefeller Centre in midtown Manhattan to obtain some information on that otherwise remote ship, operated by Compagnie de Navigation Mixte. When my teacher returned, he said that first-class accommodations on the *Kairouan* were very comfortable, that almost all fellow passengers were either French or French-speaking and that the food was quite good, at times more exotic than gourmet. He and his family repeated the African visit two summers later. This time it was more convenient – they sailed from New York to Cannes on the *Independence* and then travelled (by train) to Marseilles for a sailing on the *Ville D'Oran* to Oran. Then, ships such as the *Kairouan* and *Ville D'Oran* were quite unusual, even quite special, to me. I knew them only through Laurence Dunn's wonderfully encyclopedic first edition of *Passenger Liners*.

'The *Kairouan* is unmistakably French – everything about her is *tres chic*.' So wrote the late C.M. Squarey, who, in the 1950s mostly, reviewed dozens of passenger-carrying ships, liners and freighters for his employer, Thomas Cook. He produced monthly newsletters about his findings and these went to thousands of interested and prospective sea travellers. Expectedly, he covered the busy North and South Atlantic, Australian and Mediterranean trades, but he often went farther afield – to the more detailed Far East, the exotic Middle East and even on less familiar North and West African routes. At the time of his familiarisation voyage on the 8,500grt *Kairouan* in the

autumn of 1951, she was the 'crack ship' in the busy French services across the western Mediterranean to North Africa. Considered a true passenger ship, the 24-knot vessel was then the fastest in that service and dubbed a 'super ferry'. Her regular run was between Marseilles, Algiers and Tunis and she made it to Algiers in seventeen hours and to Tunis, in twenty-three.

Built by Forges et Chantiers de la Méditerranée at La Seyne, the 486ft-long *Kairouan* was every inch a modern vessel, another symbol of France's maritime recovery from the destruction and devastation of the Second World War. She had actually been ordered in 1939, launched during the war in 1941 and then sunk three years later by the retreating Nazi forces at Toulon. She was salvaged in 1947 under the most difficult circumstances. Listing sharply, her bow was on a 17-fathom bed while her

Fast service to Africa. The speedy *Kairouan* is seen here at Algiers. The 486ft-long ship was completed in 1950. (Richard Faber Collection)

Above: A passenger ship belonging to Compagnie de Navigation Mixte was the 1933-built, 6,000grt *El Mansour*. (Richard Faber Collection)

The smallish, 4,200grt *Djebel Dira*, built in Britain and completed in 1948, was used on the Marseilles–Casablanca run. She was designed to carry 56 first-class, 132 third-class and 430 deck-class passengers. (Gillespie-Faber Collection)

stern rested on the deck of another sunken liner, the *Virgilio*. Repaired, rebuilt and then outfitted, she finally entered service in 1950. Her owners, Compagnie de Navigation Mixte, had lost a number of their ships in the war and so this new flagship of the line was enthusiastically received. Powered by steam turbo-electric engines that were inspired by the great *Normandie* of 1935, the *Kairouan* reached a startling trial speed of over 26 knots. Painted entirely in white, she was topped by a single funnel of the then-new Strombous design – wide, tapered, but altogether extremely narrow – which was a smoke-deflecting style created by the French military. It was used on other French passenger ships and, more notably, aboard Holland America Line's new sister ships *Ryndam* and *Maasdam*.

Typically, the *Kairouan* was class-divided – 133 in first class (which in fact was subdivided as four deluxe, ten priority, forty-eight semi-luxury and seventy-one first class), 291 in tourist class and 750 in deck class. 'She is a beautifully appointed ship, in fact a little gem,' wrote the ever-observant Squarey. 'Her air-conditioned dining saloon is on the top deck and has beautifully screened glass doors as an entrance. And, of course, her kitchens are nothing short of superb.'

Surely a great improvement onexisting ships on the transatlantic shuttle, her novelties included a 'convenience' in every first- and tourist-class cabin. Adjoining each bedside, and appearing to be an extension of the dressing table, was a little cabinet. On opening the top level, water automatically flushed all sides and ran into a basin, which was equipped with good-sized clearance. When the lid was closed, the water automatically stopped. In all, it was a very sensible solution to embarrassing *mal de mer*.

Another piece of originality in this ship was the number of adjustable seats (exactly the same as those used on long-distance aeroplanes of the early '50s) on the inboard side of the rubber-covered Promenade Deck. When all the first-class berths were sold (which they often were), the Line accepted, at a reduced fare, passengers who wished to spend the night on one of these chairs. During the summers, we can only assume that a night under the stars must have been very pleasant.

The *Kairouan* was followed, in 1952, by another innovative Mixte passenger ship: the 7,600-ton *El Djezair*. The first modern passenger vessel with her funnel placed far aft, she was described in marine design literature of the time as being built in 'tanker fashion'. Credit for being the first major liner with engines and therefore a funnel aft has always been given, however, to Britain's *Southern Cross*, completed three years later.

The *Kairouan*, *El Djezair* and others in the Mixte fleet – such as the *El Mansour* and *President de Cazalet* – endured until the late 1960s when operating conditions changed. New, purposeful passenger-car ferries were coming online, the Africans themselves began operating competitive ships and the cost and mounting staff problems of running French-flag passenger ships had risen sharply. Simply, Mixte withdrew from the passenger business and ships such as the *Kairouan* went to the breakers.

Other ships in the African trades were run by the French Line, and CGT; they had no less than ten passenger ships: *Ville D'Alger*, *Ville D'Oran*, *Ville de Marseilles*, *Ville de Tunis*, *Ville de Bordeaux*, *Napoleon*, *Charles Plumier*, *Gouverneur General Chanzy*, *Commandant Quere* and *Sampiero Corso*. Chargeurs Reunis had three liners on the Bordeaux to West Africa run: *General Leclerc*, *Brazza* and *Foucauld*. Also to West African ports, but from Marseilles, were the *General Mangin*, *Jean Mermoz* and *Foch of the Fabre Line*.

12

FRENCH STYLE: SAILING WITH PAQUET

Friends from New York City were great Francophiles – they loved, often adored, all things French. This included two-dozen voyages on board the legendary *France*. But once that grand ship was retired from French service in 1974, they turned to Paquet Lines which were then running cruises. They sailed aboard the *Renaissance* and the *Mermoz*. Even if sailing, say, from Miami on a Caribbean cruise, it was all very French – lots of French passengers, French ambience, French wines and of course French cuisine. They much enjoyed Paquet and actually joined one of the last cruises of the *Mermoz*.

What the French Line was to the North Atlantic and the run to and from New York, the Paquet Line – more formally, Compagnie de Navigation Paquet – was to the colonial African trade out of Marseilles. Their all-white, multi-classed passenger ships – with exotic names like *Koutoubia*, *Djenne* and *Lyuatey* – regularly sailed in the western Mediterranean and then into the

eastern Atlantic to such ports as Casablanca, Tenerife, Dakar and Tangier. By the 1960s, however, that century-old service was changing – the French colonial links were disappearing and so went that guaranteed flow of government and affiliate passengers. Passenger-car ferries were also becoming popular and even the airlines were making a strong, competitive appearance. And so, Paquet began to seek its fortunes elsewhere in the passenger ship business.

The veteran *Koutoubia* and *Djenne* were transferred to a new subsidiary, Compagnie Francaise de Navigation, for example, and were renamed *Phocee* and *Cesaree* respectively. They were placed in the modest-price tourist and migrant trade between France and Israel. They also ran economy cruises. The new, larger *Ancerville* – with her distinctive appearance – was launched in 1962. A 14,000-tonner carrying over 700 passengers in three classes, she was still

The 10,000grt, 1952-built *Lyuatey*, used on the Marseilles–West Africa run, could do 22 knots and sometimes as much as 24 knots. The 465ft-long ship was topped by a smoke-deflecting Strombous funnel, a concept developed by the French Air Force. (Albert Wilhelmi Collection)

Transformation. Many French liners found further life as Greek cruise ships. The 1949-built *Azrou* of Paquet Lines was rebuilt in 1968 as the 500-passenger cruise ship *Melina* for the Efthymiadis Lines. (Author's Collection)

Rust and neglect. Laid up and rusting near Piraeus in Greece in a photograph dated 1976 are the Greek passenger ships *Arcadi*, formerly the French *President de Cazalet*, and behind her the *Knossos*, ex-*La Bourdonnais* of Messageries Maritimes. (Antonio Scrimali)

Four classes. The 9,500grt *General Leclerc* operated on the Bordeaux–West Africa run for Chargeurs Reunis. Built in 1951, she was typically designed for that trade with four classes of passengers – 125 in first class, 78 in second, 48 in third and 380 in fourth class. (Alex Duncan)

Exotic destinations. Built in 1951, the 9,500grt *Foch* sailed for the Fabre Line on a service from Marseilles to Dakar, Conakry, Abidjan, Takoradi, Lome, Lagos, Duala and Pointe Noire. (Gillespie-Faber Collection)

Completed in 1957, the *Jean Mermoz* was the last passenger ship for the Fabre Line and sailed in the West African trade until 1970. (V.H. Young & L.A. Sawyer Collection)

Constructed at Southampton in England, the 4,400grt *Commandant Quere* was created especially for French Line's Corsica run from Marseilles and Nice. (Albert Wilhelmi Collection)

running some West African sailings but was often diverted to cruises as well – for Carnival in Rio, to Havana and other Caribbean ports, and to the Greek isles and Black Sea. The company was encouraged by cruising and, in 1966, commissioned the splendid, yacht-like *Renaissance*, a compact 11,700-tonner that could carry 400 passengers, all of them in first class. Initially spending most of her time in Mediterranean waters on itineraries from Marseilles, she later journeyed to Scandinavia in the summer and to the Caribbean and South America in the winter. For a time, she made an annual seven-week cruise

around continental South America. She also hosted an annual 'Music Festival at Sea' cruise, featuring top classical artists in on-board performances. Fares were usually doubled, even tripled, for these very successful, two-week-long sailings. The great success of the 492ft-long *Renaissance* prompted a second ship, the 12,400grt *Mermoz*, which joined the fleet in 1970 after an extensive conversion in Italy to a cruise ship. She too had been in the old West African colonial trades, having been built in 1957 as the *Jean Mermoz* for the Fabre Line. Carrying up to 757 passengers, she also cruised on varied itineraries.

Africa bound. The *Ville de Tunis*, with a Strombous funnel, was completed in 1952 for French Line's Marseilles–colonial North Africa service. Sold in 1967, she joined the Kyriakos Lines of Greece, becoming their *City of Athens*. She sailed on the short-sea run between Piraeus and Heraklion on Crete. (Albert Wilhelmi Collection)

Modern style. The *Ancerville*, built in 1962 for Paquet Lines, could reach up to 22½ knots on the run to Morocco, Senegal and the Canary Islands. Sold in 1973, she became the Chinese *Minghua*, first used as a cruise ship and later as a moored hotel at Shenzhen. (World Ship Society)

'Typically French, the food on board the *Mermoz* was superb. There was even three bottles of wine at each table, at lunch and at dinner,' recalled the late Lewis Gordon, who cruised aboard the 527ft-long *Mermoz* from Le Havre to the Norwegian fjords and as far north as Murmansk in the summer of 1975. 'The cabins, however, were awful, even cruel and so unbelievably narrow. Mostly, there were French passengers on board who were, quite sadly, very unfriendly. There were only five or six Americans, including ourselves, on board. All the entertainment was in French, even the comedy routines. After forty years of travelling on ships, the *Mermoz* was my first sea-going exposure to topless sunbathing!'

While Paquet was later officially renamed Nouvelle Compagnie de Paquebots, they were marketed more simply as Paquet Cruises. The 10,500grt passenger-car ferry *Massalia* was added in 1971 for the last Marseilles–Casablanca sailings and then, in 1975, the 11,600grt British ferry *Eagle* became the *Azur*. That latter ship was refitted and used for considerable cruising, usually to the Eastern Mediterranean and sometimes into the Black Sea.

The promise of more of that legendary French cooking lured Lewis Gordon and his wife to the 750-passenger *Azur* for a cruise out of Toulon to Italy, Greece, Turkey and Egypt. 'Unfortunately, the ship was a big disappointment. Even though the Car Deck, the big on-board garage that once held up to 200 automobiles, had been closed, the gasoline fumes lingered and still permeated throughout the entire ship. But the biggest surprise was the food. It was not for cruise passengers. We had hamburger meat every night!'

Wanting a stronger presence in the booming American cruise trade, Paquet bought Holland America Line's 1957-built *Statendam*, a 24,200-tonner that could carry up to 952 passengers, in 1981. She was renamed *Rhapsody* and divided her time between summers in Alaska, sailing from Vancouver, and the remainder in the Caribbean, usually from Miami. She did not last very long, however, and she was sold in 1985 to Greece's Regency Cruises where she became their *Regent Star*.

Paquet, still French-owned, but now using the Bahamas flag, was finally down to one ship: the *Mermoz*. All other French liners were gone, including

Yacht-like. Carrying as few as 416 passengers in all first-class quarters, the 11,700grt *Renaissance* was a popular cruise ship offering French style, service and cuisine. (Port of Le Havre Authority)

Gathering. Four liners seen at Malta, on 10 May 1970 – Paquet LIne *Mermoz* is in the foreground, the schoolship *Uganda* of British India is behind and then the *Queen Frederica* (left) and *Taras Schevchenko* are in the background. (Author's Collection)

the likes of the French Line and Messageries Maritimes, the *Mermoz* was the last passenger liner to fly the Tricolour by 1984. Among the latter-day Paquet fleet, the *Ancerville* was sold off to the Chinese in 1973 and became their *Minghua*; the *Renaissance* changed to *World Renaissance* for the Epirotiki Lines; and finally, the *Azur* became *The Azur*, first for Chandris Cruises and then Festival Cruises.

13

LAST OF THE LINE: THE LEGENDARY *FRANCE* OF 1962

It was a cold winter's night in the early 1970s. We were visiting the great *France* along New York's Luxury Liner Row. Like kids at Christmas, we toured the ship (even after many previous visits), sat in several lounges, ordered drinks and watched the boarding passengers, often very stylish with the women clad in opulent fur coats. Well-known TV star Jackie Gleason was even said to be sailing. Bellboys carried hand luggage, often splendidly matched in fancy Louis Vuitton. Great sets of suitcases and even those hefty Vuitton trunks were being delivered to the finest cabins and suites on the ship's upper decks, and dogs, often with leather collars attached to silver leads, were being walked to the top-deck kennel. There were small but festive parties, champagne and trays of canapés almost everywhere. We braved the chilly night and briefly walked the Sun Deck. It was in itself magical – those two enormous funnels, in deep black and lipstick red, were showered in floodlighting. Steam was hissing from one and created a busy, sort of electric mood. We disembarked, looked back from the pier-side and bid our farewells. An hour later, as I returned to New Jersey and the other side of the Hudson, the *France* was mid-river. She was glittering and those twin funnels were even more radiant. Rows of windows and portholes were lit, making the enormous ship look much like a diamond bracelet laid out on black velvet. Graciously, she was moving downriver, heading for Cannes on a special late winter season crossing and to do some Mediterranean cruises. It was all so evocative. In the '60s and early '70s there was possibly no ocean liner more glamorous than the *France*. 'She was,' as one onlooker commented, 'the *Normandie* of her time.'

The *France*, the last of the transatlantic super liners that was not expected even to cruise occasionally, has left behind a glamorous, but somewhat inflated and even unrealistic, impression. Designed in the mid-1950s, for what still seemed to be a healthy trade on the North Atlantic, she sailed regally into New York Harbor on a cloudy winter's afternoon in February 1962 to cheers, excitement, praise but also some uncertainty. Could the French ever hope to recover their $80 million (£27 million) investment? Even when filled to the last upper berth, would she be profitable? Most likely not.

Just launched. The mighty *France* is moved to the fitting-out berth at St Nazaire just after launching on 10 May 1960. (Albert Wilhelmi Collection)

Although often heavily, if not fully, booked, the 66,300grt *France* was always a subsidised ship, unable to earn her keep for most of her French Line days.

Perhaps more so than Britain's subsequent *Queen Elizabeth 2*, the 1,035ft-long *France* – the world's longest liner for several decades – was the last true 'ship of state', a floating national showcase of art, design, technology, and sheer maritime engineering. To the French government, in particular President Charles de Gaulle himself, her purpose was to triumph – to very proudly fly the Tricolour. Profit was not actually to her very being. Like the super liners of the 1930s, including the *Normandie*, the profits were measured differently – in terms of prestige, goodwill and flag-waving. In these, the giant, luxurious and splendidly fed *France* succeeded beautifully. She was the most glamorous ship of her time.

Internally, the *France* – which could carry up to 1,944 passengers, 501 in first class and then 1,443 in tourist – seemed to be a series of modern and even ultra-modern public rooms, all attached to one another in a long sequence. The first-class section was dominated by a string of expensive suites, ranging from bed-sitting room arrangements to more elaborate affairs that included private verandas, dining rooms, warming kitchens, trunk and dressing rooms, and even attached quarters for personal servants. For the rich, famous and well-travelled, first class on the *France* was unsurpassable. These upper-deck passengers also had another superb amenity: the circular Chambord Restaurant, perhaps the most exquisite public room on a post-war liner to date and an amenity noted by epicure Craig Claiborne as 'the best French restaurant in the world'. As on almost all previous French liners, a large staircase descended into the room. Otherwise, particularly in tourist class, while generally spacious and always impeccably maintained, the decor tended to be either too flashy, too bright or too austere. One critic wrote, 'There are too many winged chairs on board, making the ship appear like some functional space craft.' The late ocean liner historian Frank Braynard, who attended the maiden arrival festivities, added, 'She was immediately equated with the brilliant *Normandie*, but that earlier ship was vastly superior. In the case of the new *France*, the legend exceeded the reality.'

The *France* sailed for about ten months of each year on the North Atlantic, between Le Havre, Southampton and New York. In her early years, she made only rare appearances in the Caribbean in winter and usually on rather expensive two- and three-week cruises. Later, she went off on a special cruise to Rio for Carnival and then, in 1972 and 1974, made two, widely publicised cruises around the world. Realistically, she was not the most appropriate liner for the tropics. Being basically a transatlantic 'indoor' ship, her aft Pool Deck was enclosed by glass and her upper, open-air deck spaces were rather limited.

I personally sailed on the *France* in the summer of 1973, just as the French government was beginning to seriously question her ever-increasing subsidies

Gala voyage. The *France* at Le Havre prepares for her maiden crossing to New York in February 1962. (Albert Wilhelmi Collection)

Winter afternoon. The *France* departing from New York on her eastbound maiden crossing. (Moran Towing & Transportation Company).

The *France*'s maiden departure from Pier 88, New York. The *Queen Frederica*, *Olympia* and *Carinthia* are berthed in the background of this winter scene. (Author's Collection)

Midnight sailing from Southampton. The 1,035ft-long *France* at the Ocean Terminal. (Author's Collection)

(then well over $12 million (£9 million) annually). To a new generation of politicians in Paris, it seemed a wiser choice to support Air France's supersonic Concorde instead. On my sailing, the courtesies of free wine and caviar had disappeared, there were some 500 unfilled berths and a number of souls like myself were travelling at a very affordable $150 (£105) student fare down in tourist class for the five nights to Le Havre. A former first-class waiter told me years later: 'We had almost twenty different unions on board the *France*. The on-board shop stewards were difficult and the union leaders ashore even more difficult. Behind the scenes, the *France* actually became an unhappy ship, an unpleasant place to work. This was another problem for the French Line.' A year later, in September, the government decided the *France* was simply too costly. Her 1,100 crew members reacted rather harshly. They held the ship in the English Channel and demanded a hefty 35 per cent wage increase. Their methods did little more than create a further nuisance and soon the ship was docked in the backwaters of her home port and laid up.

Dinosaur-like, many felt that the *France* might actually be scrapped and rumours were frequent. There were reports that she might become a hotel

on the French Riviera or in the Caribbean, that the Arabs wanted her as a pilgrim ship, the Chinese for a floating trade fair and the Soviets as a big floating hospital. The ship was sold finally to an Arab, businessman Akram Ojjeh, for $22 million (£16 million). He had equally unrealistic plans: converting the liner into a floating centre of French culture as well as a gambling casino and then mooring her offshore near Daytona Beach, Florida. Nothing came to pass.

It was the Norwegians who saw a bright and realistic future for the ship, however. They already monopolised the American cruise trades and predicted even better days ahead. Christian Kloster, then managing director of Oslo-based Klosters Rederi, the parent of Miami-headquartered Norwegian Caribbean Lines (later restyled as Norwegian Cruise Lines), was among those who supported the bold venture of reviving the world's longest liner as the world's largest tropic cruise ship. 'Even laid up, she was of absolutely impeccable quality,' he told me several years ago while on a cruise to the Bahamas aboard NCL's *Sunward II*. 'Everything about her – from hull plating to the engines – was top quality. After, she was the

A striking view of the *France* at Le Havre. (Albert Wilhelmi Collection)

pride of France and, to the government underwriters back then, cost was incidental. According to our marine inspection teams, she was built to last for fifty years.'

After considerable cosmetic surgery at the Hapag-Lloyd shipyards at Bremerhaven, the vastly different and renamed *Norway* recrossed the Atlantic, from Oslo to Miami via Southampton and New York. Painted externally in blues and whites, she acquired a fresh, festive quality. She had become a floating carnival of pleasures within, with a large theatre, two decks of shops, a huge casino, bars, discos, pools and even an ice-cream parlour. With her total rejuvenation costing some $130 million (£97 million), reports from Norwegian Caribbean were that she was financially profitable within three years. She was the strong, practical investment her new owners foresaw. In 1983, the *Norway* returned to Europe for further repairs and a general overhaul. In doing so, she made a rather nostalgic Atlantic crossing to Southampton, Amsterdam and Hamburg, which rekindled something of that earlier transatlantic era, of the

career of the *France*. She was decommissioned in 2003, laid up for some time and then finally towed to India and scrapped in 2009.

The *France* was by no means the last of the great French-flag passenger ships. Three notable ships that come to mind from the 1960s were the *Ancerville* (1962), *Renaissance* (1966) and, the final traditional French passenger ship, the combination passenger-cargo liner *Pasteur*, commissioned in 1966.

Until the late 1960s, Messageries Maritimes had the largest passenger ship fleet under the French flag. While their ships were far smaller and certainly less luxurious than, say, the transatlantic liners of the French Line, their passenger vessels – numbering a dozen at peak – served on far-flung, worldwide routes. In 1962, the company thought of yet another ship, a rather large passenger-cargo ship in fact, and proceeded with plans despite the emergence of jet airliners. She was to be called *Australien* and to be used on a long-haul service from Marseilles to the Caribbean, through the Panama Canal and then to the South Pacific and Australia. According to plans, this

17,900-tonner would replace an earlier pair of combo liners, the sisters *Caledonien* and *Tahitien*, which dated from the early '50s. The building order was given to Ateliers et Chantiers de Dunkerque et Bordeaux at their yard in Dunkirk. Soon afterwards, in 1963, with a sudden drop in trade on the Pacific–Australian service, plans were altered: the ship was modified for the South American trade and restyled to become the *Bresilien*. In fact, she proved to be one of the last two-class ships for Latin American service.

By the time of launching, on 2 June 1966, she had been renamed again, this time as *Pasteur*. She was to be something of a reminder of the earlier *Pasteur* (built in 1939). This new *Pasteur* was delivered in October 1966 and soon replaced all existing French combination liners on the South American trade. Her sailings were coordinated instead with an Argentine liner, the 11,400grt *Rio Tunuyan* of the ELMA Lines.

Luxuriously appointed and well designed, the 571ft-long *Pasteur* was the finest ship of her time sailing between Northern Europe and South America. Her routing, almost identical to her predecessors, took her from Hamburg, Antwerp, Le Havre, Vigo and Lisbon across the South Atlantic to Rio de Janeiro, Santos, Montevideo and Buenos Aires. A call at Southampton was introduced in February 1969, just as a long-time rival, Britain's Royal Mail Lines, withdrew from South American passenger service.

A great ocean liner enthusiast, collector and former ship's purser, the late John Havers recalled a short voyage on board the *Pasteur* in the summer of 1972:

> One of the last long-distance liners, the *Pasteur* carried 163 first class and 266 tourist class passengers as well as five holds of cargo. I travelled in her from Southampton to Le Havre, with three days ashore, and then on to Hamburg, with another three days ashore, and then back to Southampton. It was a marvellous 'coastal cruise' with ample time in ports. The outstanding memory of this voyage was the food, which was truly out of this world, even despite the 'between voyages' nature of the run and the crew taking leave where they could. With every lunch and dinner, one was given a complimentary litre of red and litre of white in labeled bottles. A formidable challenge to one's thirst! The patisserie sweets were the tastiest delicacies I have ever consumed. There were private facilities in all first-class cabins, which had a very spacious feel to them. The public rooms were straightforward modern types, clean as well as comfortable. The most used and most attractive place was the first-class bar, which was long (sixteen stools), very well lighted and nicely designed. I met a long-distance round-tripper from Germany, who made the entire voyage to Buenos Aires and back at least once a year, but did not know what he would do if the *Pasteur* was ever withdrawn.

Laid up at a Le Havre backwater between 1974 and 1979, the *France* was likened to a ghost ship – lonely, silent and all but empty. (French Line)

It was in fact only months later, in October 1972, that the *Pasteur* was withdrawn, the last deep-sea passenger ship in the once-large Messageries Maritimes fleet. A victim of a declining passenger trade and the transition to containerised cargo shipping, she was put up for sale and found a buyer immediately.

Her new owners, the Shipping Corporation of India, sent her to an Amsterdam shipyard for a refit and alterations. Renamed *Chidambaram*, she would be used, beginning in April 1973, on the low-fare run in the Bay of Bengal, between Madras and Singapore with calls en route at Nagapattinam, Trincomalee and Penang. With part of her original cargo space converted in to large dormitories, her passenger capacity was more than tripled – to 154 passengers in cabin class and 1,526 in dormitory and deck classes. Most unfortunately, on 12 February 1985, the *Chidambaram* was swept by fire while at sea and over fifty lives were lost. Ravaged from end to end by the blaze and then beyond economic repair, the ship was later brought to Bombay to await the scrapper's torch. It was a sad ending for the *Pasteur* of 1966, France's last traditional passenger ship.

The age of the great French passenger ships is not entirely over. Well into the twenty-first century, there are lectures about them, articles and books,

The 18,700grt Norwegian America liner *Bergensfjord,* built in 1956, was sold to the French Line in 1971, becoming their *De Grasse* for both the Le Havre–West Indies service as well as cruising. She was sold off very quickly, however, in 1973. Next, the 577ft-long ship became the *Rasa Sayang* for cruising from Singapore. (Author's Collection)

Last of combo era. Commissioned in 1966, the 18,000grt *Pasteur* was among the very last combo passenger-cargo liners to be built. She sailed in Messageries Maritimes' final service from North Europe to the East Coast of South America. (Roger Sherlock)

films, museum exhibits and then there is memorabilia – collectable pieces ranging from postcards to restaurant china to the smoking room chairs of these fascinating but bygone ships. In a recent and extensive sales catalogue, items continued to be diverse, interesting and often very appealing to collectors (on both sides of the Atlantic). Collectible shows have been held at Cherbourg, Le Havre and, in November 2013, at Deauville, and of course across the Atlantic in New York (where a piano from a *Normandie* suite was bought for over $100,000 (£40,000) and a quartet of Dupas glass panels from that ship's grand salon fetched over $600,000 (£250,000)). Items for sale at Deauville in November 2013 included a set of printed documents from the *L'Atlantique* selling for €70 (£50), a bronze medallion from the *La Marseillaise* for €90 (£70), an oversized company portrait of the 1966 *Pasteur* for €300 (£280), a silver serving platter from the *Brazza* at €350 (£320), a chair from the St Tropez lounge aboard the 1962 *France* at €1,000 (£800), a silk scarf by Hermes also from the 1962 *France* at €1,200 (£1,000), a classic, oversized poster dating from 1925 of the *Paul Lecat* at €1,800 (£1,600) and, on the top end, a pair of stateroom chairs from the *Liberté* at €4,000 (£3,500). Rather expectedly, some of the highest prices were for items from the great *Normandie*. A perfume decanter from Jean Patou was listed at €4,000 (£3,500), a pair of boat deck chairs was €5,500 (£4,750) and eighty-four pieces of Christofle silverware were €11,000 (£9,000). In all, French passenger liners of the twentieth century make for a very interesting group. The likes of the Île de France, L'Atlantique, Pasteur, Cambodge and Flandre are worthy of further recognition, possibly added documentation. They certainly create a nostalgic review. Indeed, what a grand cast of great ships!.

The French themselves still enjoy sea travel. In 2013, the national cruise industry was growing – over 500,000 French holidaymakers per year were taking to the seas. But there are no French-flag passenger liners these days. Club Med, Compagnie du Ponant and Paul Gauguin Cruises are considered French cruise lines even if they are no longer flying the French flag. Several other ships, including the Spanish-owned *Horizon* and *Zenith* as well as the Portuguese *Lisboa*, are specially geared for the French charter cruise market.

All in all, French passenger liners of the twentieth century make for a very interesting group. The likes of the Île de France, *L'Atlantique, Pasteur, Cambodge* and *Flandre* deserve further recognition, possibly added documentation, but certainly another nostalgic review. What a grand cast of great ships!

Two gifts to America from the French. The symbolic Statue of Liberty and the legendary *France*. (French Line)

BIBLIOGRAPHY

Baul, Patrick. *Half Century of Cruise Ships in Saint-Nazaire*. Spezet, France: Coop Breizh Publications, 2003.

Braynard, Frank O. and Miller, William H. *Fifty Famous Liners, Volumes I–III*. Cambridge, England: Patrick Stephens Ltd, 1982–87.

Dunn, Laurence. *Passenger Liners*. Southampton: Adlard Coles Ltd, 1961.

Harvey, Clive. *Normandie: Liner of Legend*. Stroud, Gloucestershire, England: Tempus Publishing Ltd, 2001.

Haws, Duncan. *Merchant Fleets: French Line*. Uckfield, East Sussex: TCL Publications, 1996.

Kludas, Arnold. *Great Passenger Ships of the World (Volumes 1–5)*. Cambridge, England: Patrick Stephens Ltd, 1972–76.

Kludas, Arnold; Heine, Frank; and Lose, Frank. *The Great Passenger Ships of the World*. Hamburg, Koehlers Verlagsgesellschaft mbh, 2006.

Miller, William H. *Classic Liners: Île de France & Liberté: France's Premier Post-War Liners*. Stroud, Gloucestershire: The History Press, 2013.

Miller, William H. *Classic Liners: SS Normandie*. Stroud, Gloucestershire: The History Press, 2013.

Miller, William H. *Picture History of the French Line*. Mineola, New York: Dover Publications Inc., 1997.

Miller, William H. *Pictorial Encyclopedia of Ocean Liners, 1900–1994*. Mineola, New York: Dover Publications Inc., 1995.

Transportation Guides, Inc. Official Steamship Guide. New York, Transportation Guides Inc. 1937–63.